IN YOUR GREENHOUSE

WITH

PERCY THROWER

In your

GREENHOUSE

with

PERCY THROWER

LONDON
W. H. & L. COLLINGRIDGE LTD

First published in 1963
by W. H. & L. Collingridge Limited
2-10 Tavistock Street, London W.C.2
Filmset and printed in Great Britain by
Photoprint Plates Ltd., Basildon, Essex
Bound in Great Britain by
Leighton Straker Bookbinding Co. Ltd., London

© Percy Thrower 1963

Second impression 1964

Third impression 1965

CONTENTS

INTRODUCTION

The cultivation of plants in a greenhouse is one of the most fascinating branches of gardening and I am sure that there are few gardeners who, at some time or another, have not had a desire to grow plants under glass.

I think that one of the most rewarding times in a greenhouse is the winter and early spring when outside the garden is dull and bleak. Even in the smallest greenhouse with a moderate amount of heat one can have a colourful display with daffodils, hyacinths, freesias and tulips. Cinerarias and various primulas, raised from seed, will also be in bloom and if one can maintain slightly higher temperatures such plants as cyclamen and poinsettias are other possibilities (the cultivation of these are all described in later pages).

For the summer there are fuchsias, achimenes and regal pelargoniums or one may prefer to grow tomatoes and possibly a grape vine. No greenhouse is complete without chrysanthemums in the autumn to be followed soon, once again, by the winter flowers.

Even without a heating system there are a great many colourful plants that can be grown in pots. The miniature cyclamen and small narcissi as well as *Primula* Wanda are all delightful in winter. Although hardy enough outside, the protection of the glass prevents the blooms being spoilt by the weather. During the summer it is perfectly feasible to grow fuchsias and tuberous-rooted begonias although they cannot be started into growth as early as those in a heated greenhouse and consequently they will be later in flowering.

It must be remembered that gardening under glass requires more skill than growing plants in the open. In a greenhouse one has to control the climate, by means of a heating system, ventilation and damping down, and it is necessary to learn how to do this to suit the plants that are being grown. Then one has to learn how to pot and water a plant and prick out seedlings. All this may seem a little frightening at first but with a little practice and good instruction it is surprising how one can soon master the art of greenhouse cultivation.

TYPES OF GREENHOUSE

Before purchasing a greenhouse one must give careful thought to the plants that are to be grown and then select a greenhouse suitable for the plants.

Span-roof. The span-roof greenhouse is perhaps the most popular kind as a wide range of plants can be grown in it. The kind with glass almost to ground level (3) is most suitable for growing crop plants, such as lettuce or tomatoes, in beds on the floor of the house and chrysanthemums in the autumn as the plants receive all the available light.

Some gardeners may only want to grow pot plants on staging and for this work a span-roof greenhouse on low

walls of brick or wood, to the height of the staging would be suitable. As a compromise between these designs, greenhouses can be obtained with glass to ground level on one side only, for growing plants in beds, and on the other side there is staging for pot plants (2).

Dutch Light Type. This greenhouse (4) will suit the gardener who is interested in growing mainly crop plants such as lettuce in winter with tomatoes in the summer. Large panes of glass admit plenty of light.

Metal Types. Several designs, made of non-rusting alloy (8) are available and with their slim glazing bars and large panes of glass they admit plenty of light.

Conservatory Greenhouse. Great interest is being shown in this type of design (7) built against the wall of a house with possible access to the living room.

Lean-to Greenhouse. Similar in some ways to the conservatory, the lean-to (5) makes use of a wall. Inside the greenhouse the wall can be used to good advantage with a trained peach or nectarine tree or perhaps a tender climber such as Passion Flower.

Three-quarter Span. Although not often seen today these greenhouses (6) have many advantages. Like the lean-to they are built against a wall but higher than it to provide a short span which will allow more light into the greenhouse. In the greenhouse shown this short span is a ventilator along the entire length of the ridge.

Siting. The positioning of a greenhouse is most important. For convenience it should be near to the house and within easy reach of water and electricity supplies, but the greenhouse must not be shaded by buildings or trees. The greenhouse and frames (1) are well placed, as they are arranged so that they receive all available light. Lean-to and three-quarter span greenhouses are usually placed against south-facing walls. North walls are not suitable as the lack of light limits the plants that can be grown successfully.

5

6

7

8

9

ERECTING A GREENHOUSE

It is possible to get a firm of greenhouse makers to erect a greenhouse of any size or pattern desired but the 'made to order' greenhouse is inevitably more expensive than one purchased in standard size sections for erection by the purchaser. As this is the way most amateurs purchase their greenhouses today it is the erection of such a greenhouse that I describe here. The particular house illustrated was made by using the sections for two standard houses bolted end to end. One was glazed to ground level on one side only, the other, a little shorter, was boarded to 2½ ft. all round. The end section was omitted from the longer house, being replaced by the door section of the shorter one. In this way a double greenhouse was obtained with dividing partition so that one compartment could be kept, if desired, at a higher temperature.

First a good foundation was made with concrete prepared with 5 parts all-in ballast to 1 part cement thoroughly mixed dry and then mixed again with water to the consistency of stiff porridge (1). The foundations were shaped by shuttering of 6 in. planks spaced 6 in. apart. When thoroughly dry bitumen damp course was rolled out on top of the concrete (2). One side section and one door section were then placed in position and carriage bolts driven through the holes prepared by the makers (3). For extra stability further carriage bolts had been partly sunk in the concrete so that they projected through holes made in the base plates. By this means the whole structure could be bolted down to the foundation. When all side, end and door sections had been bolted in position, the roof sections were slid into place (4).

5

6

Roofing and Glazing

Roofing. Each roof section was screwed to the side and middle sections already erected (5). An ornamental facia was then nailed to each end of the ridge (6).

Glazing. This was done in this instance with one of the putty-impregnated glazing tapes (7) but it could equally well have been done in the old-fashioned way with plain putty worked evenly down the rebates in the glazing bars (8). Glazing tape has the merit of being quick and easy. In either case the glass is firmly bedded on this and then glazing sprigs are driven in to hold the glass down. This is most readily done by holding a piece of flat metal, such as an old chisel, against the sprig and striking the metal with a light hammer (9). Finally the putty is worked well down into any crevices and the surplus removed (10). All glazing should be done working backwards from one end of the house to the other, one strip from bottom to ridge being completed at a time.

7

8

9

10

11

STAGING AND

Staging is not always required in a greenhouse as some crops, e.g. tomatoes, are better grown on the ground or in rings of prepared soil (ring culture—see page 117) standing on a bed of ashes or gravel. But staging is convenient for the cultivation of many pot plants and, if it is screwed or bolted together (1), can be removed when necessary. Staging may be either open, i.e. made of slats with air spaces between (1) or closed, e.g. made of cement sheeting, concrete or other solid substance usually covered with a layer of gravel or small stone chippings to hold moisture (2). For most purposes staging at one level, usually about 2 ft. above ground level, is convenient but in wide greenhouses or where displays of plants are to be arranged, it is sometimes convenient to have tiered staging at several levels (3).

Heating. Though a great deal of interest can be obtained from an unheated greenhouse it will be impossible to exclude frost from this at all times and so it cannot be a permanent home for tender plants. The range of plants is greatly increased if frost can be kept out even in the coldest weather and still further increased if a minimum temperature of 7°C. (45°F.) can be maintained. There are many tropical plants which require even higher minimum temperatures but the cost of heating a house can increase disproportionately as these higher figures are arrived at.

Methods. There are five main ways in which a greenhouse may be heated: by solid fuel, electricity, gas or oil-fired boiler or by paraffin. Solid fuel boilers to burn anthracite, coke or special fuels are probably the cheapest to operate but require the most attention. In small greenhouses the boiler is usually installed in the end wall (5) often alongside the flue. Unfortunately in such a position they are exposed to changes of wind which may affect rate of burning. This can be reduced by erecting a shelter around the boiler or building a tool or potting shed on to the end of the greenhouse to contain the boiler. Water from the boiler is usually circulated by thermosyphon action through 4 in. diameter metal pipes which must have a steady rise of about 1 in. in 10 ft. to their furthest point from the boiler

HEATING

and an equally steady fall back to it.

Oil-burning adaptors for ordinary solid fuel boilers are available (6) and may be thermostatically controlled so that they require a minimum of attention. For larger installations special oil-fired boilers are manufactured and have a very high degree of efficiency and automation.

Paraffin. No form of heating is simpler or cheaper to instal than a portable paraffin heater. It is advisable to choose one specially designed for greenhouse heating rather than to use a stove made for household use as

paraffin fumes can be deadly to some plants. The greenhouse patterns are designed to reduce to a minimum the risk of fumes and are often fitted with tubes or other devices to distribute their heat as evenly as possible (7). It is sometimes thought that paraffin heaters dry the atmosphere but the precise opposite is actually the case. As paraffin burns water vapour is produced, so that the atmosphere remains humid. Paraffin heaters should be kept spotlessly clean, and should never be turned too high and should not be stood in draughts.

Gas-fired boilers are as easy to operate as those burning oil and are equally adaptable for full automatic control by a thermostat (4). Some care should be taken to site the boiler and its flue where there is no danger of gas fumes being carried into the greenhouse for they are, if anything, even more damaging to plants than fumes from an ill-adjusted or dirty oil burner.

13

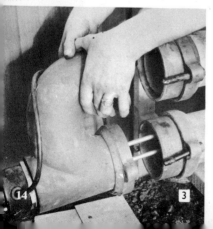

ELECTRICAL HEATING

Electrical heating may prove more costly to operate than that operated on solid fuel, oil, paraffin or gas but has the compensating advantages of ease of control, cleanliness and safety to plants. It should be expertly installed for exposed or ill-made electrical connections in the damp atmosphere of a greenhouse can be lethal.

Types. Many different types of electrical heating apparatus have been developed for greenhouses. Tubular heaters (1) have much the same capacity for even distribution of heat as hot water pipes. They may be installed in single lines or banks according to the degree of heat required. The usual loading is 60 watts per ft. of tube.

A more compact heater is the fan-assisted type (2). That illustrated has a loading of 3,000 watts, i.e. equivalent to 50 ft. of tubular heaters but is quite small and can be readily moved about. The hot air is pushed to all parts of the greenhouse.

Another alternative is to use an electric immersion heater to warm water which is then circulated in pipes just as it would be from a boiler. The model illustrated (3) is designed to slip into ordinary 4 in. diameter water pipes, thus eliminating the need for a boiler. It embodies a thermostatic control.

Thermostat. All forms of electrical heating may be controlled thermostatically and special thermostats are available for greenhouse use. The most sensitive is the rod-type thermostat and it should be mounted as nearly as possible in the middle of the house where it will register the mean temperature. It is an advantage to shield the rod from direct sunlight by silver foil as this will enable the thermostat to give a more accurate reading of air temperature.

SOIL WARMING

Considerable advantage is to be gained with some crops by warming the soil from below and this also hastens the rooting of cuttings and the germination of seeds.

The most convenient way of warming the soil where a mains electricity supply is available is electrically. There are two major alternatives: either low voltage current, reduced from the mains voltage by a transformer, can be passed through bare wires or the full mains voltage can be passed through insulated soil warming cable. In either case wire or cable should be buried 4 to 6 in. in the soil.

The pictures show the installation of a mains soil warming cable. Shorter lengths of cable are available.

Laying Wires. First the soil is excavated to the required depth and a good layer of sand is scattered over the bottom. This should be raked level. Next the required length of cable, to be ascertained from maker's recommendations, is spread evenly over the whole surface in lines as nearly parallel and equi-distant as possible (1). Small, hairpin-like pegs of bent galvanised wire will be found useful to hold the cable in position.

With low voltage wire there is no need to take any special precautions to protect the wire, but mains cable can be dangerous if it is accidentally severed by a spade, trowel or other tool. To guard against this it is an excellent plan to lay a length of galvanised wire netting right over the cable (2). More sand is thrown over this and then the soil is replaced (3). The cable should be plugged into a waterproof switch socket provided for it in a convenient place, preferably well above soil level where it is unlikely to be accidentally splashed with water.

Thermostats. It is possible to obtain soil warming cables complete with built-in thermostats so that the current is automatically switched off when the soil temperature rises above a certain point. This is useful and economical but not essential as the loading of these cables is never very high—usually enough to provide a temperature of about 16°C. (60°F.).

TEMPERATURE CONTROL

Insulation. The amount of artificial heat needed to maintain a greenhouse at any desired temperature can be reduced by proper insulation of the side walls and also by eliminating all cracks through which cold air may enter or warm air escape. Wooden-sided houses are particularly in need of extra insulation and this may be done with glass wool, asbestos packing or any other heat insulating material.

Lengths of glass wool, of a kind commonly used by builders for insulation, may be placed against the wood on the inside of the house (1). They can then be held in place with pieces of asbestos-cement sheet cut to fit (2). This adds further to the insulation and also protects the woodwork from wet.

Electrical heaters and gas or oil-fired boilers can be controlled quite easily by means of a thermostat installed inside the greenhouse. The thermostat can be set at any desired temperature (3) and will then turn off the heating when the temperature rises a trifle above the figure and turn it on again when the temperature falls a trifle below it. There are several different types of thermostat but the rod type illustrated (3) is the most sensitive. It should be placed as centrally as possible and a little above the level of the plants so that it registers the free air temperature of the house.

Thermometer. A thermometer that can be set to register maximum and minimum readings is almost a necessity as it enables the gardener to check on the performance of the heating apparatus and thermostat and make certain that nothing is going wrong in his absence. Some thermometers are set with a magnet (4) others by tilting them up.

SHADING AND VENTILATION

During the summer most greenhouse plants, with the exception of cacti and other succulents, will require some shading from direct sunlight. The simplest way to provide this is to paint the glass on the south side of the house with whitewash (1). Plain whitewash made with lime and water will wash off fairly quickly but if just a little size is added, it will adhere much better. An alternative is to make use of one of the proprietory shading compounds.

Blinds. The drawback to coating the glass in this way is that the shading is permanent and cannot be altered to suit changing conditions. This is where blinds that can be lowered or raised at will have an advantage. Fabric or polythene blinds can be used but if they are to be fitted outside the house, it is better to have blinds made of wooden laths (2) or split cane.

Ventilators. Ventilation is required to change the air in the house and keep the temperature from rising too high. If hinged ventilators are used there should be some mounted high near the ridge (4), to let hot air out and some in the sides to let cool air in, especially when the weather is very hot. The aim should be to maintain a fairly steady temperature, but higher by day than at night.

Electric fans can also be used for ventilation (3) and if controlled by a thermostat can be completely automatic in operation.

WATERING AND DAMPING DOWN

Watering cans are supplied with roses which may be fine or coarse (1). These are only needed when watering seeds, cuttings, or very young plants. Established plants should always be watered direct from the spout of the can, but this should be held close to the soil so that the water does not force out the soil (2). Sufficient water should be given at each application to soak right through the soil in the pot. As a rule no more will be needed until the soil begins to get dry. Appearances in this matter can sometimes be deceptive. One way of checking the amount of moisture in a clay flower pot is to rap it with something hard such as a cotton reel pushed on to the end of a stick or cane (2). If the pot gives out a hollow or ringing sound the soil within is dry; if it sounds dull and heavy it is wet. With a little practice considerable accuracy can be attained.

Damping Down. Moisture is needed in the air as well as in the soil but the amount required varies with different plants. Succulents like a much dryer atmosphere than ferns or foliage plants. Air moisture can be supplied from evaporating trays, also by watering paths and under staging (3) and by syringing between the pots (4) or even over the leaves of plants that like a lot of moisture. This is known as 'damping down' and may need to be done two or three times a day in hot summer weather.

WINTER CLEANING

Light. In winter most plants require all the light they can get so if limewash or other 'permanent' shading has been put on the glass it should be removed (1). In any event it will be wise to wash down all the greenhouse glass both inside and out to remove dirt and grime. A long-handled broom is useful for this and warm water containing a little detergent will soon loosen the dirt.

The most difficult place from which to remove dirt is in the overlaps between panes of glass. A special tool may have to be made for this purpose from a strip of thin metal slightly bent, as shown in the illustration (3), so that it can be slipped in between the panes and drawn from side to side.

Woodwork and Walls. These should also be scrubbed to get rid of dirt and any lurking insect eggs (2). A little disinfectant added to the water will help. This work can be done more easily and safely if the plants can be removed temporarily. One advantage of doing this work in winter, generally immediately after the last chrysanthemums have flowered and been cut down, is that this is usually the time when the greenhouse is least crowded. If walls are of concrete or brick it will help to limewash them (4) after they have been scrubbed down. Freshly made limewash will help to destroy pests and fungus spores and, by reflecting light, will improve the illumination of the house.

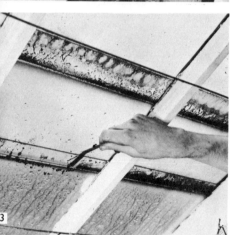

CLEANING AND FUMIGATING

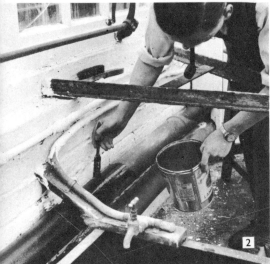

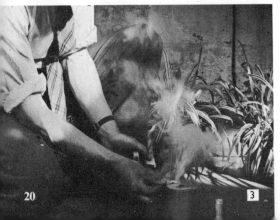

Heating Pipes. If greenhouses are heated by water, the water pipes must also be attended to annually. First use a wire brush to remove rust and scale (1). Then the pipes can be painted with some old sump oil into which a little lamp black has been stirred (2). This is not simply a matter of appearances or of preserving the pipes from rust. Heat will be more efficiently radiated from pipes that are clean and black than from those that are scaled and rusty.

Control of pests and diseases must continue throughout the year though winter often affords the best opportunity to have a thorough clean up. Dusts and sprays such as are used outdoors can also be employed in the greenhouse and many chemicals are available which are specially effective against this or that pest, e.g. DDT against white fly, BHC and menazon against greenfly and azobenzene against red spider. However, there is one technique of pest and disease control peculiar to the greenhouse and notably convenient and efficient there, namely fumigation.

Fumigation. Sometimes this is done by evaporating a liquid such as nicotine over a small spirit lamp; sometimes by vaporizing a chemical such as sulphur in a special apparatus so designed that the sulphur cannot ignite and produce fumes deadly to all plant life. But the simplest method of fumigation is by means of special smoke generators which are rather like small fireworks. A generator of suitable size (or more than one generator if necessary) is placed low down in the house in a central position and ignited (3). It emits dense clouds of smoke which carry the particular chemical contained in the generator to all parts of the house. Generators of various sizes are available containing most of the well-known insecticides, BHC, DDT, etc., and there are also fungicidal generators for use against diseases. The amount of space for which each generator is effective will be printed on it or on the container in which it is purchased.

Fumigation is best done towards evening. All ventilators should be closed and the house vacated immediately and not be re-entered for several hours. Make sure the chemicals are not harmful to the plants.

SEED AND POTTING COMPOSTS

Loam. Seeds are germinated and plants are grown in mixtures, usually of soil and other ingredients, known as composts. The most generally useful of these are those known as John Innes Composts for which there are two basic formulae, one for seeds, the other for potting. Both these make use of loam, a term rather loosely used for soil that contains some clay, sand and humus. The definition of the loam needed for John Innes Composts is medium, neither too heavy (clay) nor too light (sand) with a pH of 6.5 or thereabouts. One way of providing loam is to obtain turves cut thickly with two or three inches of soil from a good meadow or building site. This should be stacked, grass side downwards (1) and left for some months (as much as a year if possible) so that grass and root fibres may decay.

Peat. The second bulk ingredient for the John Innes Composts is horticultural grade peat which should be granular and reasonably free from dust. As purchased this is usually very dry and dry peat resists moisture. As it is essential to get the peat moist before use it should be spread out and liberally watered (2). It may be necessary to repeat this several times, turning the peat after each watering and then spreading it out again.

Sand. The third bulk ingredient is sand, defined for this purpose as coarse and sharp, with particles grading up to ⅛ in. in size. Cornish river sand is ideal (3).

It is not essential to make these composts at home as they can be purchased ready mixed. If obtained from a thoroughly reliable source there is considerable advantage in this, but some dealers offer so-called John Innes Composts which bear little resemblance to the genuine article and there can be no guarantee that these will give satisfactory results. If in doubt, therefore, it seems best to secure the right ingredients and mix them oneself. It is not particularly difficult but the loam should first be sterilized by standing it over boiling water in a saucepan or copper or in one of the special sterilizers which can be purchased for the purpose. The ideal is to raise all the soil to a temperature of 93°C. (200°F.) and maintain it at that for 20 minutes.

MIXING COMPOSTS

The John Innes Seed Compost is prepared by mixing 2 parts loam, 1 part peat and 1 part sand, all parts by loose bulk. To each bushel of these combined ingredients is added $1\frac{1}{2}$ oz. superphosphate of lime and $\frac{3}{4}$ oz. of either finely ground chalk or limestone. First the loam is passed through a $\frac{1}{2}$ in. mesh sieve to remove stones (1). Then the peat and sand are added and finally the chemicals, carefully measured out, are scattered over the top (2). The whole heap must then be turned several times (3).

The John Innes Potting Compost is prepared in a similar manner but the proportions of the main ingredients are different: 7 parts loam, 3 parts peat and 2 parts sand. A base fertilizer is added to this. It can be purchased ready mixed or can be made with 2 parts of hoof and horn meal, 2 parts superphosphate of lime and 1 part sulphate of potash, all parts by weight. This is added to the other ingredients at the rate of 4 oz. per bushel for No. 1 Compost, 8 oz. per bushel for No. 2 Compost and 12 oz. per bushel for No. 3 Compost. To No. 1 add $\frac{3}{4}$ oz. of finely ground chalk or limestone per bushel of mixture; double and treble this amount for Nos. 2 and 3. The No. 1 Compost is used for all ordinary purposes, No. 2 Compost for older plants in pots over 4 in. diameter and the No. 3 Compost for some very strong growing plants in 10 in. pots.

SEED SOWING

Preparation. Seeds can be sown in ordinary flower pots, special seed pans or shallow seed boxes such as that illustrated on this page. A convenient measurement for such boxes is $14\frac{1}{2}$ in. by $8\frac{1}{2}$ in. by 2 in. There should be a slit or other outlet for water in the bottom and this should be covered with pieces of broken pot, known as crocks. Then the box is filled with prepared seed compost (1). The compost must be made evenly firm all over and this is done first by pressing it in with the fingers (2) and then using a special wooden block fitted with a handle to make it quite smooth, level and firm (3). This block, known as a 'patter', can be made quite easily at home. When firmed ready for sowing, the level of the compost should be $\frac{1}{4}$ to $\frac{1}{2}$ in. below the sides of the box.

Exactly the same care must be taken in preparing seed pots or pans for sowing and similar provision must be made for drainage. If surplus water cannot drain easily out of the soil, seeds will rot and seedlings will be killed.

Before sowing, the compost should be well watered in (4). For this purpose use a watering can fitted with a fine rose and be careful not to flood the soil out of the box.

Seed must be sown evenly and thinly. There are many ways of doing this and it is possible to buy seed sowers of various

23

patterns. However, one simple and quite effective method with seeds of reasonable size is to pour some from the seed packet into the palm of one hand, take small pinches of seed from this with the other hand and scatter them over the surface of the compost (5).

Covering. The seed is covered with the same compost as that used in the box or other receptacle. It can be sprinkled carefully by hand but an easier and safer method is to scatter it through a rather fine sieve (6). One can be made for the purpose with a small wooden box, the bottom of which has been replaced by a piece of perforated zinc. Depth of covering will vary according to size of seed. The very finest seeds, such as those of begonia and gloxinia, require no covering at all as they will fall between the particles of soil. Fairly large seeds, such as those of marigolds, may be covered with $\frac{1}{4}$ in. of soil.

Every sowing should be carefully labelled not only with the name of the seed but also with the date of sowing. At first it is convenient to lay the label flat against one side of the box (7). This is to enable the whole box or other receptacle to be covered with a sheet of paper—old newspaper will do excellently (8). The purpose of this is to exclude light until the seed germinates but directly the first tiny seedlings can be seen coming through the soil this covering must be removed.

PRICKING OUT

After germination the seedlings must be given as much light as possible to keep them sturdy. As soon as they can be handled conveniently, which is usually just as they are about to produce their first true leaves as distinct from their seed leaves, they must be transplanted to other boxes, a process known as pricking out.

The boxes are prepared exactly as for seed sowing and as a rule the same seed compost is used but occasionally, for strong growing plants, a richer compost is used, such as John Innes Potting Compost No. 1.
The Seedlings. These are very carefully lifted, one at a time, from the seed box (1). A sharpened wooden tally makes a good tool for this and it is important to have the soil in the right condition, nicely moist right through, neither too wet nor too dry. Hold each seedling by one seed leaf and transfer it immediately to the box in which it is to be pricked out. Make a small hole for it with a wooden dibber, drop the roots straight down into this (2) and press the soil around them with the dibber. The seedlings should be spaced approximately 2 in. apart in straight rows so that each has enough room to grow on into a sturdy little plant.

When the box has been filled with seedlings it should be well watered to settle the soil still more around the roots. Once again a watering can fitted with a fine rose is required to do this thoroughly yet without damage (3).

LABELLING AND SOIL BLOCKS

The boxes in which the seedlings are pricked out must also be labelled clearly and for this purpose I have shown a different method which is equally applicable to seed boxes. Part of the top of one end of the box is pared smooth with a knife (1) smeared with white paint (2) and then the particulars are written on the still moist paint with a lead pencil (3).

Soil Blocks. These provide an alternative method both of germinating the larger seeds and of pricking out seedlings. The blocks are made of ordinary seed or potting compost compressed in a special mould. Several types of mould can be purchased, some extremely simple others more complex and capable of handling big quantities. Each block of moulded soil contains a small depression into which a seed or the roots of a seedling can be dropped (4). Then a little more soil is run over the seed or around the roots of the seedling and is made firm with the fingers (5). The blocks are stood side by side in boxes and are well watered (6).

HANGING BASKETS

Although hanging baskets are usually seen outside in summer they can also be used for a display inside a greenhouse.

Plants that are most suited to cultivation in baskets have a pendulous habit. Fuchsias (1) are ideal but some varieties are better than others. A few good ones are Powder Puff, Trail Blazer, Lilibet and Enchanted. Pendulous begonias also look lovely in hanging baskets as well as the popular Busy Lizzie (*Impatiens sultanii*). Plants that are used for baskets outside in the summer are ivy-leaved pelargoniums, trailing lobelia, *Campanula isophylla*, *Asparagus sprengeri* and petunias.

The wire baskets are made in various sizes but those of 12 or 14 in. in diameter are likely to look more impressive, when the plants are in full flower, than those of smaller size.

Preparation. The time to prepare hanging baskets is in early spring and to keep the basket steady whilst it is being prepared it can be stood on a pot. The basket should be lined thickly with moss (2) to hold the potting soil—John Innes Potting Compost No. 1 is suitable. It should be added a little at a time as the moss lining is built up. The small plants, such as variegated nepeta or lobelia, can be pushed through the wires in the sides of the baskets (3) as the potting soil is added so that the whole basket is well clothed with foliage and flowers. When the basket is well lined with moss and the soil has been firmed with the fingers (4) the top of the basket can be planted. Ivy-leaved pelargoniums can be placed at an angle (5) so that the new growth will hang over the sides of the baskets.

To allow space for watering at the top of the basket a rim of puddled clay can be made around the top wires. The baskets can remain standing on pots in the greenhouse or better still they can be hung up on a stout beam. To encourage a compact bushy habit the tips of fuchsia stems should be nipped out frequently (6 and 7); premature flowers also should be removed. The plants soon fill the baskets with roots and watering must be attended to carefully as the soil tends to dry out rapidly, particularly when the weather is hot and dry.

HANGING BASKETS *continued*

Feeding. I am sure that many people fail to obtain the best from plants in baskets because they neglect to feed them at regular intervals. Soluble fertilizers can be given every 7-10 days in the summer and it will help the plants to go on flowering well into the autumn.

Propagation. To have well rooted plants ready for the baskets in the spring, cuttings of fuchsias and ivy-leaved pelargoniums should be taken in July and August; the rooted cuttings can be over-wintered in 3 in. pots. Pendulous begonias are started into growth in the same way as the large flowered tuberous begonias, details of which are given on page 35. Lobelia is best raised from seed each year.

28

ACHIMENES

With flowers in shades of pink, purple, scarlet and white, achimenes is another excellent plant for a hanging basket (1), although it is more often seen as a pot plant. Its common name is Hot Water Plant because it is supposed to benefit from being watered with hot water. This is not true and watering can be done in the same way as for any other plant.

Starting. The small scaly rhizomes (2) are started into growth in early spring by pressing them into moist peat and sand (3) in pots or boxes in a temperature of 13-16°C. (55-60°F.). New growth soon develops and the young plants can be moved to 5 in. pots; several can be grown in a 5 or 6 in. pot spacing them 2-3 in. apart. In hanging baskets the small plants can be pushed gently through the wires in the side of the basket so that eventually the basket is hidden with flowers and foliage. Plants grow well in John Innes Potting Compost No. 1.

Watering. At first watering should be done sparingly but as growth develops it should be increased. As soon as the roots begin to fill the pots feeds of a soluble fertilizer can be given with benefit. The stems need supporting as they tend to be straggly but all that is necessary is a few twiggy sticks inserted around the edge of the pot. Light shade should be given from strong sunshine and to avoid a dry atmosphere when the weather is hot, floors and staging should be damped frequently.

Resting. The foliage will show signs of withering in early autumn and at this stage less water should be given until the soil is quite dry. The rhizomes can remain in the pots for the winter provided they are kept in warm, dry conditions. Then in the spring the contents are tipped out and the rhizomes started into growth once more.

1

2

3

4

APHELANDRA

A plant that has become popular as a room plant in recent years is *Aphelandra squarrosa louisiae* (1). I think of it as a dual purpose plant because it has handsome dark green leaves with prominent white veins and cones of bright yellow bracts surrounding the flowers at the tips of the stems.

Although plants can be used in rooms for short periods they grow best in a greenhouse with a minimum temperature of 13°C. (55°F.) in winter.

Propagation. Plants can be increased readily from cuttings and young unflowered side shoots, a few inches long, should be selected (2). The lower leaves should be removed (3) and a clean cut made below a joint at the base. To assist rooting the lower ends of the cuttings can be dipped in a hormone rooting powder (4) and I like to place the cuttings individually in small plant pots (5). A suitable rooting medium consists of 1 part loam, 2 parts moist peat and 3 parts coarse sand. This should be firmed around the cutting (6) and then given a good watering (7). The pots may be placed in a propagating box with a temperature of 18-21°C. (65-70°F.) or each pot can be enclosed in a polythene bag (8).

Potting. The rooted cuttings are first moved to $3\frac{1}{2}$ in. pots using John Innes Potting Compost No. 1 (9) and later to 5 or 6 in. pots of J.I.P.2.

5

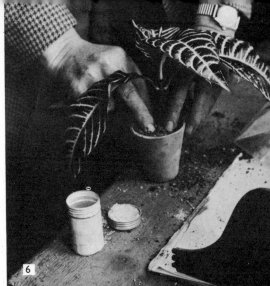

6

The growing tips can be nipped out when the plants are in 5 in. pots to produce plants of a bushy habit.

Feeding. Once plants are established in their final pots, feeds of a soluble fertilizer at 10-day intervals will help keep them growing well. As they come into flower the plants are best kept in cooler conditions.

The lower leaves tend to fall as the plants age, particularly if they are kept in a room for too long where the air is hot and dry. In these circumstances it is best to cut back the stems in the spring and, given warmth and moisture, new growths soon develop. These can be removed as cuttings if one wishes when they are a few inches long.

7

8

9

ARUM

The correct name for this plant is *Zantedeschia aethiopica*, although it is often wrongly referred to as richardia. The pure white spathes (1) on long stems surrounding the true flowers are much in demand at Easter for flower decorations.

Starting. The time to start plants into growth is in July or August when the old soil should be shaken from the roots. At this stage they can be divided (2) and about three roots or crowns can be accommodated in an 8 in. pot (3). John Innes Potting Compost No. 2 can be used and it must be worked well amongst the roots. After a good watering the pots should be stood in a sheltered place in the open but taken into a light place in a cool greenhouse before the end of September. Until growth begins water should be given sparingly. The temperature can be raised gradually to 13-16°C. (55-60°F.) as the plants develop if early flowers are needed but the plants will be quite happy in a temperature of 7-10°C. (45-50°F.) if flowers are not needed too early.

Feeding. Arum lilies respond to feeding and once the pots are full of roots regular feeds of a soluble fertilizer will help to produce good flowers (4).

Resting. After flowering, watering and feeding must not be neglected but in early June I like to give the plants a rest by laying the pots on their sides in the open (5) so that the soil is kept dry until repotting is done once again in August.

Greenfly can spoil the flowers but fumigation with nicotine shreds will soon deal with them. If reddish globules are seen on the underside of the foliage the presence of thrips must be suspected. The use of a DDT smoke bomb will control these insects. As a precautionary measure it is probably best to use a combined DDT-BHC smoke cone which will destroy both thrips and greenfly.

AZALEA

Indian azaleas (1) with their colourful flowers can be seen in most florists' shops in the winter and early spring and if one has a cool greenhouse, and the plants are given a little attention, they can be kept for many years.

Potting. After flowering is over the remains of the withered flowers should be removed (2) and the plants repotted. Rhododendrons and azaleas will not tolerate lime or chalk in the soil and so a special potting mixture must be used. This can be made by mixing 2 parts of moist peat with 1 part coarse sand. The old drainage crocks must be removed from the base of the plants (3); the fresh potting soil is worked around the roots (4) and firmed well with the fingers (5).

Watering. The peaty soil must never be allowed to dry out; if this happens it is extremely difficult to get it properly moist again. New growth soon begins after flowering and it is best to keep the plants in a warm part of the greenhouse; sprays of water over the plants will help to encourage good growth. In districts where the tap water is hard and contains lime it is wise to use rain water for these plants.

From June until September the plants can with benefit be plunged outside in their pots (6). It is best to choose a position in partial shade as they do not like strong sunshine.

Feeding. As the potting soil contains little

AZALEA *continued*

plant food it is necessary to feed the plants regularly so that they make good growth and flower well. Nowadays there are numerous liquid or soluble fertilizers that can be obtained from garden shops. One can use a dry feed of 2 teaspoons full of dried blood to 1 of sulphate of potash for each plant. This can be given every 14 days in the spring and summer.

Watering must be attended to each day when the plants are in the open during the summer, although the compost in the pots will not dry out so rapidly when the pots are plunged in ashes or soil. Overhead sprays of water are also beneficial.

As the nights become colder in September the plants should be returned to a cool greenhouse (7). Although high temperatures are not needed, sufficient heat should be turned on to keep the air fairly dry otherwise the blooms will be spoiled by dampness.

Propagation. The Indian azaleas that are imported to this country from continental sources, to be forced in time for Christmas, are usually grafted plants.

Grafting is a highly skilled job but new plants can be raised from cuttings. It takes longer to produce a sizeable plant by this method but it is a simpler procedure than grafting. Young shoots, that have begun to harden at their base, are selected and inserted in small pots of moist peat and sand. The pots should be stood in a warm, moist propagating box until rooted.

BEGONIA

There are numerous kinds of begonia with colourful flowers or attractive foliage that can be grown without difficulty in a heated greenhouse but the ones that are most popular are the tuberous rooted kinds. These have large double flowers (1) and few people can help admiring their beauty. Apart from these there are the tuberous pendulous begonias which are seen at their best when grown in a hanging basket (2). This variety is called Golden Shower.

Propagation. Tuberous begonias can be grown from dry tubers, which can be purchased in named varieties, and seed is obtainable from begonia specialists. However, unless one has a greenhouse with a heated propagating case, where a temperature of 18-21°C. (65-70°F.) can be main-

tained, it is better to grow the plants from tubers. Seed sown in January or February will produce plants for flowering in mid-summer. John Innes Seed Compost can be used and the seed, which is very fine, should be sown carefully on the prepared compost in a pot or pan. As the seed is so fine I like to mix it with fine sand before sowing to ensure even distribution. After germination and when water is needed, I think it is best to hold the pot in a bucket of water (3) until the moisture percolates through to the surface.

Starting Tubers. Dormant tubers can be started into growth in March and the plants will flower in late June onwards. The tubers, hollow side uppermost, can be pressed into boxes of moist peat and coarse

BEGONIA *continued*

sand (4) and kept in a warm part of the greenhouse with shade from strong sunshine. Light sprays of water overhead will help new growth to develop but care must be taken not to overwater, particularly in cold weather. When the new shoots are a few inches tall (5) the plants can be removed and placed in 5 or 6 in. pots, according to the size of the plant; John Innes Potting Compost No. 2 is a suitable mixture to use.

Seedlings. Once the seed has germinated the seedlings must be pricked out in boxes to allow $1\frac{1}{2}$ in. between each small plant. As they are very small and rather difficult to handle a small forked stick can be used to transfer them to the dibber holes in the box. The tiny plants must be kept in a temperature of 18°C. (65°F.) and given shade from strong sunshine. When large enough their next move is to 3 in. pots (6) of J.I.P.1. and they can then be treated in the same way as the plants from tubers.

Final Potting. The final move for seedling begonias, when their roots have filled the 3 in. pot with roots, is to 5 or 6 in. pots using J.I.P.2. (7). Good drainage with plenty of crocks in the bottom of the pot is necessary and after potting a cane can be inserted in the pot and a tie given with raffia (8).

Disbudding. The first flowers that appear should be removed so that the plant makes good growth before the flowers open. Later on it is wise to do some disbudding. It will

9

10

11

be noticed that the flowers usually appear in threes. Beside the male double flower there will be two female flowers on either side. The latter produce poor flowers and should be pinched out (9) to leave each double flower to open to its full size. As the plants develop the stems must be tied carefully and it pays to give support to the flower stems as the blooms are rather heavy (10).

Botrytis, the grey mould fungus disease, can be troublesome on begonias. It often makes an appearance in cold, damp weather or in an insufficiently ventilated greenhouse. The fungus may gain an entry through broken leaf stalks. Any withered leaves should be removed with a sharp knife close to the stem and if the disease appears it pays to dust immediately with flowers of sulphur (11).

Watering. Begonias need to be watered carefully as overwatering can result in poor growth. Water should be given sparingly after potting and until new roots are made into the fresh compost. Each plant must be treated individually and when the soil in the pot is beginning to dry out the pots should be filled with water. Water must not be given again until the soil shows signs of dryness once more.

Feeding. As the plants become established in their final pots, feeds of liquid manure at intervals of 7-10 days can be given with benefit—the John Innes Liquid Feed is very good.

Resting. Tuberous begonias must not be dried off too quickly. I like to keep the

12

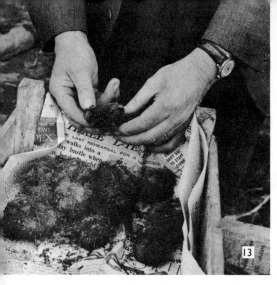

13

14

plants growing for as long as possible into the autumn but when the foliage shows signs of yellowing, watering can be reduced and the plants laid on their sides under the greenhouse staging (12). When the stems have withered completely the tubers can be removed from the pots and the old soil shaken out (13). They can then be dusted with flowers of sulphur (14) and stored in boxes of dry peat, sand or old potting soil in a dry, frost-free place until it is time to start them into growth again in the early spring.

Rex Begonias

These are grown primarily for their handsome leaves as the flowers are not very showy. They have fibrous roots and should not be dried off at any stage. They like a greenhouse with a minimum temperature in winter of 10°C. (50°F.) with shade from strong sunshine in the summer. Although it is not the best place for them I have often seen plants placed partly under the greenhouse staging.

Propagation. These begonias can be pro-pagated from their leaves. The conventional method is to sever a leaf (15) with a piece of stalk attached and then to slit the veins on the underside of the leaf with a sharp knife (16). It is then laid on the surface of a peat and sand mixture in a pan or shallow box. Small stones laid on the leaf (17) help keep the cut veins in contact with the rooting medium. Stood in a warm, moist propagating box with a temperature of 16-18°C. (60-65°F.) rooting soon occurs.

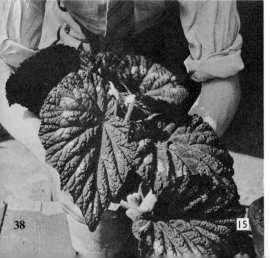

15

16

Another method is to cut the leaves in small squares and to place them on a mixture of moist peat and sand in a shallow box. They are then treated as for whole cuttings.

Potting. The small plants are first moved to 2 in. pots and then to $3\frac{1}{2}$ and 5 in. pots. When the young plants are established in their final pots feeds with a liquid or soluble fertilizer will help the plants (18).

Lorraine Begonias

These are fibrous rooted winter-flowering begonias and they are really delightful when covered with masses of flowers. Gloire de Lorraine with pink flowers is the most popular variety but there is also a white one called Turnford Hall. Their stems are more wiry than the large-flowered tuberous begonias and the plants are more graceful. To grow them well a temperature of at least 16°C. (60°F.) is needed.

Cuttings. To obtain young basal growths

for cuttings the stems of the plants are cut back to within a few inches of their base after flowering (19). Kept in warm conditions new shoots soon develop and these can be removed in February as cuttings (20).

A suitable mixture for rooting the cuttings consists of 1 part loam, 2 parts moist peat and 3 parts coarse sand. The ingredients must be well mixed together and 3 in. pots are filled with compost.

Each cutting is prepared by trimming the

LORRAINE BEGONIAS *continued*

base immediately below a leaf joint, with a sharp knife or razor blade (21). Several cuttings can be placed around the edge of a 3 in. pot using a dibber (22) and after a good watering (23) the pots of cuttings should be stood in a propagating box—a temperature of 18°C. (65°F.) is desirable.

Potting. The rooted cuttings are first put in 3 in. pots (24) using John Innes Potting Compost No. 1 and firming the soil lightly. In a temperature of 16-18°C. (60-65°F.) and a moist atmosphere growth is made rapidly. Shade must be given from strong sunshine in the spring and summer. As the plants develop a further move to 5 in. pots will be required—these will be the final pots in which the plants will flower (25).

Staking. Thin canes inserted in the pots are needed to support the fragile stems. These are held loosely to the canes with thin pieces of raffia and it should be done so that eventually the canes are hidden and the plant is a well arranged mass of flowers and foliage.

CACTI AND SUCCULENTS

1

The cultivation of cacti is a fascinating hobby and most kinds will succeed in a greenhouse with a minimum temperature in winter of 7°C. (45°F.). During the spring and summer temperatures can be allowed to rise to 18-21°C. (65-70°F.) with sun heat, provided ample ventilation is given. Those shown, on the right (1) at the rear, are *Notocactus haselbergii* (left) and *Mammillaria kunzeana* (right). In the front are *Rebutia marsoneri* (left) and *Rebutia kessleriana* (right). Others that flower at an early age are *Aporocactus flagelliformis* (Rat-tail Cactus), *Chamaecereus silvestrii* (Peanut Cactus) and *Lobivia famatimensis*.

Cacti are sun lovers and they need the lightest part of the greenhouse. They can, if desired, be stood in a sunny cold frame

for the summer, preferably with the pots sunk in a bed of ashes.

Potting. The time to pot cacti is in the spring just as new growth is beginning. John Innes Potting Compost No. 1 can be used with the addition of 2 extra parts of coarse sand and 2 parts crushed brick. Cacti must never be placed in pots that are too big. They should be moved to pots only slightly larger than the ones in which they have been growing. Handling the plants can be difficult, because of the spines, and it is wise to make a paper collar which is placed around the plant to serve as a 'handle' (2 and 3). The old crocks and some of the old soil can be removed carefully with a pointed stick and the plant may then be placed in its new pot. The new compost can then be worked

2

3

4

41

around the ball of the roots (4) and firmed.
Watering. Growth is made in the spring and summer and during this period plenty of water is needed (5) but in winter when the plants are resting the soil must be kept dry. Watering in the winter should be necessary only if plants begin to shrivel.

Christmas Cactus

The botanical name for this plant is *Zygocactus truncatus* (6) although it has been variously referred to as phyllocactus and epiphyllum. It is a popular plant as it flowers during the winter, usually in time for Christmas. The colour of the flowers is a deep pink and they appear at the ends of the leaf-like segments. The habit of growth is pendulous and pieces of zygocactus are often grafted on to another upright cactus, such as pereskia, to make a standard plant.
Cuttings. The usual method of propagation is by cuttings taken in the spring. These should consist of several stem segments (7) and they root readily if inserted in small pots containing a mixture of 1 part loam, 2 parts moist peat and 3 parts coarse sand (8). Several cuttings can be placed around the edge of a 3 in. pot and when rooted (9) each plant should be potted individually in a 3 in. pot (10).
Potting. A suitable potting mixture consists of 2 parts fibrous soil, 1 part sieved leaf mould, 1 part moist peat and 1 part coarse

8

9

10

sand to which can be added 3 oz. of hoof and horn meal, 3 oz. of superphosphate of lime and $1\frac{1}{2}$ oz. sulphate of potash per bushel of the mixture.

Watering. Unlike many other cacti, zygo-cactus must not be allowed to dry out in the winter although much less water is needed at this time. In the summer the plants in their pots can be plunged in a bed of peat or ashes in a cold frame. The soil must be kept amply moist and light over-head sprays of water will encourage good growth. Light shade should also be given from strong sunshine.

During the summer when the plants are established in their pots feeding can be done with a liquid or soluble fertilizer every 10 days. In September the plants must be re-turned to a cool greenhouse. Flowering can be hastened a little by raising the temperature provided the air is kept fairly moist with light sprays of water.

The Christmas Cactus can be grown in a living room if conditions are suitable. A moderately heated room is sufficient and a place where temperatures fluctuate should be avoided. This can cause buds to drop; stem segments may even drop if watering is neglected and temperatures vary too much.

Echeveria

Although not often seen, *Echeveria retusa* with coral-red flowers and attractive blue-green foliage is an excellent winter-flowering succulent plant for a cool greenhouse. It is easy to grow and nearly all parts of the plant can be used as cuttings. After flowering, rosettes of leaves with a piece of stem can

11

CACTI AND SUCCULENTS *continued*

be removed (11) and trimmed at the base with a sharp knife (12). These will soon form roots if they are placed in small pots of coarse sand (13) and they will make handsome plants in the following winter.

Stem Cuttings. Another way of propagating these plants is to cut the old flower stems into pieces a few inches long (14). Several of these cuttings can be placed in small pots which should be labelled with the name of the plant (15). When rooted the plants need potting on until they are in 5 or 6 in. pots of John Innes Potting Compost No. 2. The stems should be staked neatly as they develop (16).

CALCEOLARIA

The bright and gay colours of the greenhouse calceolarias with their curious, pouched flowers always attract attention in the spring (1). Plants can be raised easily from seed and the time for sowing is in July to produce plants for flowering the following May. The seed should be sown on the surface of sifted John Innes Seed Compost; no further covering of soil is required. The pots should be covered with a sheet of glass (2) and stood in a cold frame. After germination the seedlings should be pricked out into boxes (3) and before the plants become too large they can be moved to 3 in. pots of John

Innes Potting Compost No. 1. In October another move to 5 in. pots can be given.

During the winter the plants are happy in a minimum temperature of 7°C. (45°F.)—they do not like high temperatures—but the air must be kept fairly dry by careful ventilation. Watering must be done sparingly otherwise plants may damp off.

Final Potting. I like to give the plants another move to 6 in. pots (4) in February to obtain really good specimens. This is well worth doing if there is sufficient space available in the greenhouse.

Feeding. As the flower buds begin to show regular feeding with a liquid fertilizer (5) will benefit the plants considerably.

Greenfly are often a nuisance on calceolarias and as soon as the first signs of the insects are seen fumigation with nicotine shreds or BHC smoke pellets should be done; instead, a systemic insecticide that is available to amateurs can be used.

CAMELLIA

Although camellias are hardy enough and they can be grown in sheltered places in the open they are also fine flowering shrubs for a greenhouse from which frost can be excluded. So often the blooms are damaged by the weather in the open but under glass they are able to develop to perfection. The kinds most commonly seen are the varieties of *C. japonica* (1).

Cuttings. One way of increasing these plants is by removing leaves, each with a bud and portion of stem attached (2). The time to do this is in March and the cuttings are

inserted around the edge of a 3 in. pot filled with a mixture of 2 parts coarse sand and 1 part moist peat (3). After a good watering the pots are stood in a warm, moist propagating box. As the roots form, new growth will develop and the young plants should be lifted carefully with a dibber or label and potted individually (4). A 3 in. pot is a suitable size and for potting use a peaty compost of 2 parts moist peat, 1 part lime-free soil and 1 part coarse sand (5). Young plants will be happy in a cold frame with shade from strong sunshine in the summer.

Cuttings can also be taken in late July but these are made from shoots made in the current season that have begun to harden at

their base. They should be treated in a similar manner to the other cuttings.

Potting. When the plants begin to fill the small pots with roots it is time to move them to 6 in. pots (6) using the same peaty compost; finally the plants, when they have become sufficiently large, can be grown in 10 in. pots or tubs.

Complete repotting of established plants is not necessary each year but when required the time to do it is in early spring just before new growth begins. The new pots must be well crocked (7) as good drainage is important and a layer of rough peat added (8). The old crocks and some of the worn out soil can be removed (9) and the fresh compost is worked around the roots (10). This is made firm with a rammer (11).

During the summer the plants are best stood outside in a partially shaded place and they must never be allowed to become dry at the roots. If this happens the flower buds are likely to drop off later. Feeds of a liquid or soluble fertilizer each week will help to keep the plants growing steadily through the summer and in hot weather overhead sprays of water will keep the plants in good condition.

In early autumn they should be returned to an unheated greenhouse that is ventilated fully. A little heat can be turned on in cold weather but too much heat must not be given. Damp, stuffy conditions must be avoided at all times and the ventilators should be kept open whenever the weather is favourable.

CHLOROPHYTUM

The Spider Plant, *Chlorophytum comosum variegatum* (1), is so named because of the rosettes that develop on the ends of the flowering stems. It is an easy plant to grow in a cool greenhouse and it will also do well as a room plant. It is grown mainly for the attractive green and cream-striped foliage. The flowers on long arching stems are insignificant but they are soon followed by the rosettes of leaves which add to the decorative value of the plant.

Propagation. As plants age and decline in vigour the rosettes of leaves can be detached (2). These are in fact small plants and root initials are usually present. If they are placed in small pots of good soil (3) new roots will soon develop (4) and they can be moved to 5 or 6 in. pots.

Indoors, it may be more convenient to place the offsets in the top of a jar of water into which new roots soon develop.

Chlorophytums have tuberous root systems and another way of increasing the plant is to separate the tubers and pot them individually.

The plants soon use up all the goodness in the potting soil and to keep them growing steadily, once they are established in their final pots, it pays to feed regularly with a liquid or soluble fertilizer.

CHRYSANTHEMUM

There are few plants that can provide so much colour in the greenhouse during the autumn as late flowering chrysanthemums. They do not require high temperatures but some form of heating is necessary to overcome cold, damp conditions which can spoil the blooms. The plants can be grown in pots throughout their life or they can be planted outside for the summer. These are lifted carefully in early autumn and replanted in a greenhouse border. I prefer to have my plants in pots as the roots are not disturbed when the plants are housed.

Varieties. There are a bewildering number of varieties for flowering from October until the end of the year and new ones are constantly appearing. They are classified by the National Chrysanthemum Society

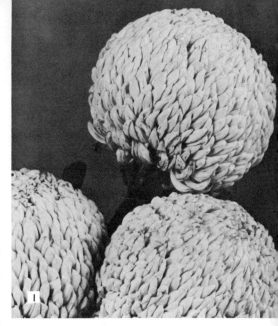

according to flower formation and time of flowering. The incurve types (1) have almost globular blooms with tightly packed petals. The reflexed varieties have blooms with outward pointing petals and they include varieties with reflexing outer petals and incurving inner petals. Then there are single varieties, which deserve to be grown more, as well as the pompons and anemone-centred chrysanthemums.

Heat Treatment. Part of the reason why new varieties are constantly being produced is that stocks gradually lose vigour. Virus diseases can cause this weakening and there is no cure for it. However, specially heat-treated chrysanthemums can be obtained. The treatment is a very specialized business and it is not possible for an amateur to do it himself. Treated plants must be obtained from a specialist chrysanthemum nurseryman.

Stools. After flowering the stems of the best plants of each variety should be cut back and having shaken off some of the old soil (2) the stools are packed closely in boxes of good potting soil (3). Kept in a light place in a cool greenhouse new shoots soon develop around the base of the old stems and they are used for cuttings (4) which can be taken during January and February.

Preparing Chrysanthemum Cuttings

Sturdy shoots only should be used. They must be short jointed and about 3 in. long. The lower leaves are removed and each cutting is trimmed below a joint at the base (5) with a sharp knife. To assist rooting the base of each cutting can be dipped first in water and then in hormone rooting powder (6). This is particularly useful for shy-rooting varieties.

A suitable rooting mixture consists of 1 part loam, 2 parts moist peat and 3 parts coarse sand which should all be well mixed. The cuttings can be inserted around the edge of a 3 in. pot (7) filled with the rooting medium or they can be put direct in a prepared bed of sandy soil inside a propagating box. From the time the cuttings are taken it is most important to label them with the name of the variety as they can so easily become mixed and as each pot is filled with cuttings it should be labelled (8). Afterwards a good watering should be given (9). A propagating box can be made simply with the sides of a large box. The top is covered with panes of glass and in the bottom there can be a layer of weather ashes or peat on which to stand the pots (unless a special bed of soil is made for the cuttings).

Potting Chrysanthemums

First Potting. The cuttings will root well in a temperature of 7°C. (45°F.)—high temperatures are not needed. Unless there are bright spells of sunshine it should not be necessary to shade the cuttings with newspaper but the glass must be removed each day (10) so that condensation can be wiped away. Little water should be needed but the compost in the pots must not be allowed to dry out. Remove any leaves that wither and after a while look out for signs of rooting by tapping out the cuttings from the pot (11).

Compost. The first potting is done in 3 in. pots (12) and John Innes Potting Compost No. 1 can be used. A crock should be placed over the drainage hole followed by a little rough peat before the compost is added. This should be made moderately firm around the roots (13). After potting give the plants a good watering (14) and stand them on the staging, well spaced out and in full light. They should be encouraged to grow sturdily by keeping the temperature around 7°C. (45°F.), opening the roof ventilators each day unless there is severe weather or fog. The plants can be moved to a cold frame in March, provided material is available, such as sacking or straw, to cover the frames on cold nights—if the frame is heated so much the better. Watering must be done carefully. After potting little water will be needed until new roots develop and in cold weather it is best to keep the soil on the dry side.

10

11

12

13

POTTING CHRYSANTHEMUMS *contd.*

Stopping. This simply involves removing the tip of the plant (15) to induce side shoots to form. This is not always necessary as some varieties 'break' or produce side stems naturally. These will produce flower buds at their tips in due course and they are called first crown buds. Some varieties however, mainly the late flowering ones, are given a second stopping to induce more side growths to develop. The buds that form on these growths are called second crown buds.

It is not possible to generalize on the subject of stopping and each variety must be treated individually. Most chrysanthemum specialists, however, give stopping dates in their catalogues and these should be followed unless one varies them slightly in the light of one's own experience.

Second Potting. As the roots begin to fill the 3 in. pots with roots (16) the plants must be potted on to 5 or 6 in. pots. Before potting give the plants a good soaking. Crocks must be removed and for this potting use J.I.P.2 compost. The young plant is placed centrally in the new pot (17) and the compost must be firmed well around the ball of the roots (18 and 19) to leave about 1 in. of space at the top of the pot for watering. Label each pot with the name of the variety (20) to prevent them becoming mixed. Afterwards return the plants to the frame and give little water for the first few days after watering. As the plants become established in their new pots open the frames fully by day to

encourage good sturdy growth.

Final Potting. This is usually carried out in early June as the roots begin to fill the 6 in. pots. For this potting use clean 8 in. pots and place a layer of crocks and roughage in the base (21) for drainage. Make sure the plants are well watered a little while beforehand. The plant is put in the centre of the pot and the new compost—J.I.P.3—is used (22). This must be made firm with a rammer (23) and space must be left in the top of the pot to allow for top dressing later with fresh compost. Do not forget to transfer the label to the final pot (24).

Staking. It is convenient at this stage to stake the plants. One method which I follow is to place three stout bamboo canes in each pot (25). A tie with raffia can then be given by looping it around the three canes (26). If the raffia is soaked in water it makes

CHRYSANTHEMUMS *continued*

it easier to use. Staking in this manner will keep each plant secure until further ties are needed. During the summer tying should be done regularly to prevent the shoots being broken by strong winds.

Standing Out. The plants are stood in rows outside for the summer and it is best to have the pots on an ash base or on pieces of slate so that worms cannot get into the pots. To keep the plants secure, wires are stretched at a height of about 4 ft. between stout posts (27) and the canes are tied to the wires with strong twine.

Feeding. As the plants develop and before they fill their final pots with roots a top dressing of fresh potting compost can be given (28) and later regular feeding with a

dry (29) or liquid fertilizer will be necessary to keep the plants growing steadily. Feeding must be done only when the compost in the pots is moist otherwise the fertilizer can scorch the roots of the plants. After applying a dry fertilizer, water it in well afterwards (30).

Watering. During the summer the plants must be inspected at least once a day to see whether they may need watering. In very hot weather water may be needed two or three times in the course of a day. Tapping the pots with a wooden hammer as described on page 18 is an old, well-tried method of testing for dryness.

Spraying. Chrysanthemums, like other cultivated plants, are likely to be attacked by pests and diseases. Regular spraying (31) with a suitable insecticide or fungicide will prevent most of the trouble. Capsid bugs, leaf miners and aphides are common pests. These can all be checked with a BHC insecticide. Mildew is one troublesome disease which causes a white powdery deposit on the foliage; it can be checked with karathane, either as a spray or as smoke under glass. Another fungicide that can be used is sulphur which can be dusted on the plants.

Side Shoots. The young growths that form in the joints of the leaves (32) on the flower stems must be removed as they appear except for varieties grown for sprays. This can be done with the fingers or with a sharp knife. Disbudding is also necessary to leave one bud on each stem, the surplus buds being removed when quite small with the fingers (33).

POTTING CHRYSANTHEMUMS *contd.*

Housing. During the latter part of September, when the nights become colder and frost can be expected, the plants must be taken into the greenhouse. Before this is done any dead and shrivelled leaves on the lower part of the plants should be removed (34). The canes can then be untied from the wires and plants carefully laid on their sides so that they can be given a thorough spraying with a combined insecticide and fungicide. They should then be free from pests and diseases before being taken into the greenhouse (35). Plants must not be overcrowded when they are housed (36) and the ventilators should be kept fully open whenever the weather permits. A little heat turned on at night in the autumn will help to keep the air circulating.

CINERARIAS

Anyone with a greenhouse, with sufficient heat to maintain a minimum temperature in winter of 7°C. (45°F.) can grow cinerarias and their brightly coloured daisy flowers give a wonderful splash of colour in late winter and early spring. In small greenhouses it is probably best to grow the Nana Multiflora strains, which grow about 15 in. tall. My favourites are the Large-flowered Grandiflora hybrids (1) that have large flowers and grow about 2 ft. tall. Even taller are the Stellata cinerarias that have a branching habit and masses of small flowers.

Sowing. Seed can be sown in April, May and June to provide a succession of bloom; plants from an April sowing should flower in December or January. John Innes Seed Compost is suitable and for the later sowings the seed pans or pots can be stood in a cold frame and covered with glass and paper. These must be removed as soon as the seedlings appear and when large enough to handle (2) they must be pricked out (3) in boxes of John Innes Potting Compost No. 1. Keep the young plants in a light place but give shade from strong sunshine.

Potting. Before the seedlings become over-crowded in the boxes move them individually to 3½ in. pots using J.I.P.1 compost. Water the boxes thoroughly before disturbing the plants and, provided the potting compost is moist, no water need be given for a few days after potting. The final potting is in

CINERARIAS *continued*

5 or 6 in. pots of J.I.P.2 compost (4). Care must be taken to see that the soil level in the pots is kept about 1 in. below the rim of the pots to allow for watering. Potting should be done as soon as the roots begin to fill the small pots. At all stages of potting adequate drainage must be provided in the pots with broken pieces of pot and a little rough peat or loam fibre.

Cool Conditions. Cinerarias do not like high temperatures and for the summer they are best kept in a cold frame, preferably standing or plunged in a bed of ashes to prevent rapid drying out. The plants must be given shade from the sun otherwise they will soon wilt and watering must be attended to carefully. Greenfly can be a nuisance and at the first signs of the insects the plants should be sprayed with a suitable insecticide.

Stopping. The tops of some of the plants can be pinched out (5) if it is desired to delay flowering and so provide a longer display of flowers. Stopping should not be done until the plants are established in their final pots.

Feeding. This is necessary to keep the plants growing steadily throughout the late summer and autumn and one of the liquid or soluble fertilizers on the market diluted in water can be used. Feeding should cease as the flowers appear (7).

In late September the cinerarias must be taken into the greenhouse (6) and arranged so that each plant has plenty of room on the staging. Ventilate freely whenever the weather is favourable. When temperatures are low watering must be done very carefully. If the soil is kept too moist the stems may rot.

The cineraria is a perennial but it is best treated as an annual by raising new plants from seed each year.

COLEUS

The handsome leaves of *Coleus blumei* are to be had in a variety of colours (1). Plants are grown for their lovely leaves and the flowers, which are not very decorative, are pinched out whenever they appear (5). To grow coleus well a minimum temperature in winter of 10°C. (50°F.) is needed. In lower temperatures, or if plants receive a check in growth, they are likely to drop their leaves. Provided a warm greenhouse is available coleus are not difficult to grow.

Propagation. The usual method is by taking cuttings of young side shoots, a few inches long (2), from mature plants. These root without difficulty throughout the spring and summer. The lower leaves are removed and each cutting is trimmed below a leaf joint at the base (3). They should then be inserted in small pots of sandy soil and placed in a propagating box with a temperature of at least 16°C. (60°F.). Young plants have the most colourful foliage and it is wise to take cuttings several times in the summer so that there are always young plants available as the older ones are discarded.

Coleus can also be raised from seed but the foliage of most of the seedlings will be of poor colour—only the ones with well-coloured leaves should be kept. These can then be propagated from cuttings each year.

Potting. Rooted cuttings are first put in 3 in. pots of John Innes Potting Compost No. 1 and later moved to 5 or 6 in. pots. Shade must be given from sun in the summer and when temperatures are high a humid atmosphere should be maintained by damping the floors and stagings in the greenhouse.

The tips of the shoots should be nipped out at intervals (4) to induce a bushy habit otherwise the plants will be badly proportioned.

CROTON

Another plant that is grown for its colourful foliage is the croton (codiaeum) (1). The leaves are thicker and the plant is more woody than the soft-stemmed coleus. The colouring of the foliage varies with the form or variety and there are also interesting variations in the shape of the leaves. Some are long and strap-like while others are more rounded in shape.

To grow crotons successfully a greenhouse where a minimum temperature in winter of 13°C. (55°F.) can be maintained is required; in summer temperatures can rise up to 24°C. (75°F.) with benefit provided a humid atmosphere is maintained by damping down inside the greenhouse. The colour of the leaves is more intense in good light but it is wise to provide some shade from very strong sunshine.

Air Layering. As plants age they tend to lose their lower leaves and the best way of obtaining young plants with foliage down to soil level is to air layer an older plant. This is done by making a cut, about 1 in. long, part way into a stem to form a tongue (2). The cut surfaces are then dusted with a hormone rooting powder (3) and the wound is surrounded with moist sphagnum moss (4). This is enclosed with a piece of polythene sheeting (5) and tied at the top and bottom with raffia or twine. The polythene prevents moisture evaporating and the moss remains moist.

Potting. A watch should be kept on the layer and when new roots can be seen twin-

ing amongst the moss the new plant can be severed from the parent plant (6) just below the new root system.

The roots at this stage (7) are rather brittle and they must be handled carefully (the moss has been removed here to show the root development). It is best to put the new plant in a 3 in. pot of John Innes Potting Compost No. 1 (8) without removing the moss and keep it in a warm part of the greenhouse so that it will make new roots. Later the plant can be moved to a 5 or 6 in. pot of J.I.P.2.

Cuttings. Instead of air layering plants, cuttings can be made from the ends of young shoots. Not too many of the lower leaves should be removed otherwise the new plant will have a bare piece of stem at the base. Cuttings root without difficulty in pots of sandy soil if they are placed in a propagating box with a temperature of 18-21°C. (65-70°F.).

Feeding. Crotons soon fill their final pots with roots and to keep them growing well they should be fed each week with a dry or liquid fertilizer; if the former is used make sure it is watered in well.

Pests. A careful watch should be kept on the plants for signs of such insects as mealy bug and red spider mites—the latter increase rapidly in the hot conditions which crotons enjoy. Regular sponging of the foliage (9) with a white oil emulsion insecticide will help to keep the plants clear of these pests and it will also enhance the appearance of the foliage.

CUCUMBER

Few people do not appreciate cucumbers for salads and they are well worth growing if a minimum temperature of 16°C. (60°F.) can be maintained.

Sowing. Seed can be sown singly in 3 in. pots of John Innes Potting Compost No. 1 (1) and the seedlings will appear within three or four days in warm, moist conditions. Before the plants fill the pots with roots they should be planted out in a bed on the greenhouse staging or in large pots (2) filled with good potting soil such as J.I.P. 3. If planting out has to be delayed it is wise to move the plants from their 3 in. pots to 5 in. pots to prevent them being starved. To support the plants, horizontal wires must be provided to support the stems.

Training. The main stem of each cucumber is allowed to grow until it reaches the top wire before the tip is removed. Side stems or laterals will form and the tips of these should be removed two leaves beyond the first fruit (3). The shoots should be tied carefully to the wires (4) and sub-laterals must all be kept stopped at two leaves beyond the first fruit. All male flowers must also be removed (5) to prevent fertilization of the female flowers.

Shade is needed from strong sunshine and copious supplies of water are required as the plants develop. Plants in beds can be top dressed with fresh potting compost when white roots appear on the surface of the beds and feeds of a suitable fertilizer will maintain good growth. If the plants are grown well, fruit can be cut within 12 to 14 weeks of sowing the seed.

CYCLAMEN

A wonderful display of colour can be had with cyclamen from the autumn until the spring and it is one of my favourite pot plants. To grow plants well they must have a minimum temperature in winter of 10°C. (50°F.). Plants are raised from seed and there are strains available with pink, red, white, violet and crimson flowers. There are also types that have frilled edges to the petals (2) which are charming companions for the usual kinds (1).

Sowing. My cyclamen seed is sown in June but sowing can also be done in August to provide plants for flowering at the end of the following year. Some gardeners sow in

CYCLAMEN *continued*

January but at this time of the year it is often difficult to provide sufficiently high temperatures, which are necessary for germinating the seed.

The seed should be spaced out evenly on the surface of a pot or pan of John Innes Seed Compost (3), and after firming the covering of sifted compost (4) newspaper is put over the pot (5) to prevent rapid drying out of the compost. Wipe the condensation off the glass daily. The coverings should be taken off as the seed germinates and the pan stood in a warm shaded part of the greenhouse.

Pricking Out. As soon as the seedlings are large enough they can be lifted carefully with a dibber (6) and pricked out in boxes of John Innes Potting Compost No. 1. This must be done before the seedlings have made too many roots (7). Some seedlings may take several weeks longer to germinate than others and so the seed pan should not be discarded until the required number of seedlings have appeared. The seedlings must be held by their seed leaves (8), to avoid bruising the delicate stems, and spaced out at about $1\frac{1}{2}$ in. apart.

First Potting. New growth is soon made in warm, moist conditions with shade from the sun and before the seedlings become overcrowded in the boxes they must be moved to $3\frac{1}{2}$ in. pots (9). Cyclamen must

have a well-drained compost and it is important to use really coarse sand. For this potting J.I.P.2 is suitable. The new pots must have good drainage with pieces of broken pot and each young plant should be placed centrally in the pot but not too deeply (10). The potting compost is made firm around the roots with the fingers (11) to leave space at the top of the pot for watering. In winter a temperature of 10-13°C. (50-55°F.) is adequate and the plants can be stood on a greenhouse shelf so that they have plenty of light.

Final Potting. As the plants fill their pots with roots (12) they should be transferred to their flowering pots. I put the strongest plants in 6 in. pots and weaker ones in 5 in.

space should be left between each plant. Overhead sprays of water are beneficial and the frame lights can be removed altogether at night.

Watering. After potting, little water will be required for the first few days but as new roots are made regular attention to watering must be given, particularly when the weather is hot. Feeds can be given at weekly intervals but only when the pots are filled with roots and more nourishment is needed to keep the plants growing steadily.

Housing. Towards the end of September and before the arrival of hard frosts the cyclamen must be returned to a frost-free greenhouse.

CYCLAMEN *continued*

pots. Care must be taken to see that each plant is placed centrally in the new pot (13) and the tuber or corm is just kept above soil level (15). The new compost (J.I.P.2) must be made moderately firm (14).

Frames. During the summer, cyclamen like cool conditions and the best place for them is in a cold frame (16) where shade can be given from the sun. To reduce watering to a minimum it helps if the pots are sunk in a bed of ashes in the frame and plenty of

As this is done each plant can be inspected and dead leaves cleared away; it is also wise to scrub any pots that have developed a green slime. If there should be any signs of greenfly spray the plants thoroughly with a good insecticide. Keep the greenhouse well ventilated and on warm days damp the floors and stagings with water to maintain a humid atmosphere (17).

Small cream-coloured grubs are often found feeding on the roots of cyclamen (they also attack tuberous begonias). These are the grubs of the vine weevil. The use of a BHC insecticide will destroy them and

where this insect pest is troublesome it pays to dust the potting compost as it is made up with BHC or aldrin.

Ventilation. As the weather becomes cooler and there is less heat from the sun ventilation must be done very carefully to avoid damp and stuffy conditions in the greenhouse. Sufficient heat should be turned on to keep a steady temperature of at least 10°C. (50°F.) at night. Should signs of the grey mould fungus appear, which is common where conditions are too damp, a fungicidal dust can be applied with a small puffer (19). Any leaves that shrivel must be removed as botrytis often starts to develop on a damaged leaf (18).

Removing Flowers. The first flowers usually appear in early autumn but I remove these until the main 'flush' of flowers develop. The way to remove the flower is to hold the stem with thumb and first finger and give a sharp tug (20). The stems should then come away cleanly without leaving a piece at the base which could rot and cause trouble later on.

23

24

CYCLAMEN *continued*

Watering must be done very carefully in the winter (22). The compost must not be kept too wet otherwise the base of the flower and the stems will rot. Tapping the pots as described on page 18 will give an indication of whether the soil is dry. When applying liquid fertilizers care should be taken to see that none of the liquid reaches the leaves or scorching may occur (21).

As the flowers fade they should be removed by giving the stems a sharp tug so that the plant does not waste energy in producing seed.

The best plants can be kept for another year and once flowering has finished they should be put to one side in the greenhouse where they can continue growing for a while. During the summer the tubers should be allowed to rest by withholding water, although I do not think it wise to dry them off completely as it is very often difficult to start dry tubers into growth again.

Watering can begin again in July and if plants are sprayed overhead with water it will help to encourage new growth.

Potting. As young leaves appear the plants should be repotted. All the old leaves should be cleared away (23) and the plants tapped out of their pots. Some of the old soil can be scraped away (24) so that the plant can be put in a clean pot of the same size— a 6 or 7 in. pot. Fresh J.I.P.2 compost is used for potting (25). Every care should be taken not to bury the tuber and it should be kept slightly above the level of the compost.

The plants soon grow away if they are stood in a shaded cold frame and given similar treatment to younger plants. Watering should be done sparingly after repotting but once roots have been made more water will be needed. The plants should come into flower at about the same time as those raised from seed. I do not think it is worth keeping cyclamen plants for more than two years. After this period they seem to lose vigour and the best results are obtained from vigorous young plants.

25

DAFFODILS
AND
HYACINTHS

Plenty of colour can be had in a warm greenhouse from Christmas until the spring with daffodils and hyacinths (1). Varieties must be chosen carefully for the earliest flowers. The dainty and graceful Roman hyacinths should not be forgotten as they naturally flower earlier than the large-flowered hyacinths. Good early narcissi are Paper White and Grand Soleil d'Or.

Treated Bulbs. Matters have been made easier for the gardener in the past few years as specially treated bulbs can be obtained that flower earlier than they would normally. Varieties of narcissus that can be obtained for Christmas flowering include Carlton, Golden Harvest, Cragford and Peeping Tom, one of the *cyclamineus* hybrids. Treated hyacinths in white, blue, red and yellow can also be obtained.

Potting. Bulbs should be potted in September

5

6

7

DAFFODILS AND HYACINTHS *contd.*

and October as soon as they can be obtained. In pots John Innes Potting Compost No. 1 can be used and the bulbs may be placed close together but so that the tips are above the level of the soil (2). It is not wise to have hyacinths of mixed colours in the same bowl as they are not likely to flower together. Bulbs may also be grown in bowls of bulb fibre but it is most important to soak the fibre thoroughly in water before it is used. The compost or fibre must not be made too firm under the bulbs otherwise the developing roots may push the bulbs out of the soil.

Plunging. The pots and bowls must be stood in a cool place after potting the bulbs for 8-10 weeks so that the bulbs can make good root systems. I find it best to stand the pots outside in sheltered places and after a thorough watering (3) cover them with a layer of sand (4) or weathered cinders. If the pots are given a long label this stands out above the covering and makes it easier when selecting varieties for taking indoors.

Lifting. The pots and bowls can be lifted when the bulbs have made plenty of roots (5) and moved to a cold frame (6). This is done so that they can gradually become acclimatized to warmer conditions and for the shoots to turn green. The bulbs can be taken into the greenhouse (7) or a light room

8

9

10

at intervals. At first a temperature of 7°C. (45°F.) is adequate and the bulbs should not be put straight into a high temperature —it should be raised gradually. Treated bulbs need slightly different temperatures but instructions are given with bulbs obtained from good bulb merchants.

Watering. The soil in the pots must be kept uniformly moist and where bulb fibre is used care must be taken to see that it does not dry out. Water must not be splashed about and if it collects inside the leaves of hyacinths the buds may rot (8).

Staking. The large flowers of the modern hyacinths are heavy and it is wise to stake them. Hooked pieces of wire (9) are un-obtrusive but canes with ties of raffia can be used. It also pays to provide some support for narcissus foliage (10) with thin canes and raffia looped around them to enclose the foliage.

Bulbs in Water. The old method of growing hyacinths in special jars has become popular once again. Top quality bulbs should be obtained and the jars are filled so that the water level is just below the bulbs. A few pieces of charcoal in water will help to keep it 'sweet'. The jars should be placed in a cool, dark position and when the shoots are a few inches high they can be taken out and gradually given more light.

Recently I have been using plastic bowls for growing hyacinths in water. The bulbs are placed on a tray which fits inside the bowl (11). Roots soon develop in cool conditions (12) and as necessary, water is replenished through a hole in the centre of the tray (13).

After Flowering. When the flowers fade the bulbs need not be thrown away, although they will not be suitable for forcing the following year. The pots can be stood in a cold frame and in early spring the bulbs may be planted in the open in good fertile soil.

11

12

13

73

DRACAENA

Grown for their handsome and colourful foliage dracaenas are hot-house plants needing a temperature in winter of at least 13°C. (55°F.) and rising to 24°C. (75°F.) in the summer. They thrive in a hot, humid atmosphere. *D. terminalis* (1) is now correctly called *Cordyline terminalis* and has numerous varieties with foliage variously tinged rose, green and white. *D. fragrans victoriae* (2) is even more showy with handsome green and cream striped leaves. As dracaenas age they tend to lose their lower leaves and if young plants are propagated each year these can take the place of the older ones which may have grown too tall. **Propagation.** There are several ways of increasing these plants. *D. indivisa* can be

5

6

7

raised from seed but special forms or varieties must be propagated from cuttings. Pieces of stem can be cut in lengths and if these are placed in a warm, moist propagating box in sandy, peaty soil dormant buds will soon develop to form new plants. Another method is to take root cuttings or 'toes' (3) from the plants. These are cut off with a sharp knife (4) and placed in small pots containing sandy, potting soil (5). The best time for taking these cuttings is in the spring and summer and in the warmth of a propagating box new growth soon develops (6).

Potting. The young plants are moved first to a 3 in. pot of John Innes Potting Compost No. 1 and until they are growing away well they should be kept in the warmest part of the greenhouse. Later they can be potted on to 5 and 6 in. pots. After removing pieces of fleshy roots the plants must be repotted. Some of the old soil will have been shaken from the roots and it should be possible to accommodate the plant in the same sized pot (7). Use J.I.P.2 compost and firm it well around the roots (8).

When the weather is hot in the summer the plants benefit if they are syringed with water—rain water is best as hard tap water will mark the foliage. Light shade should also be given from strong sunshine. Once the pots are full of roots, water should be given liberally with regular feeds of liquid or soluble fertilizer.

8

FERNS

A few ferns are invaluable in a greenhouse for their decorative foliage. Although not a true fern I am including asparagus here. The two kinds commonly grown are *A. plumosus* which has fine feathery foliage and *A. sprengeri* with needle-like foliage. Both are easy to grow and they can be raised readily from seed sown in pots in the spring. The young seedlings should be put first in 3 in. pots and later moved on to 5 or 6 in. pots. Plants of *A. sprengeri* also look most attractive when grown in hanging baskets.

Division. Mature plants may be divided by pulling the roots apart (1) in the spring. Each piece is potted in a 5 in. pot of John Innes Potting Compost No. 1 (2).

One of the popular true ferns is *Pteris cretica* with handsome light green fronds. This can also be increased by dividing an established plant in the spring (3) and potting the pieces individually.

Bulbils. One fern, *Asplenium bulbiferum*, produces small plants or bulbils on the veins of the fronds. These can be removed and laid on the surface of a mixture of 2 parts moist peat and 1 part coarse sand in a seed box (4). The bulbils can be held close to the compost in the box with bent pieces of wire. Kept moist and in a temperature of 16°C. (60°F.) roots soon develop and the small ferns can be potted in 2 in. pots of J.I.P.1 compost.

1

2

3

FICUS

The Rubber Plant, *Ficus elastica* (1), with
large dark green leaves has become a popular
room plant in recent years although it has
been grown in warm greenhouses for a long
time. I like to grow the plants in a greenhouse with a temperature of at least 13°C.
(55°F.) and take them into a room for short
spells at a time for decoration.

Air-Layering. As plants age they tend to lose
their lower leaves and become rather leggy.
To obtain a new plant from the old one it
can be air-layered. This is best done in the
spring and summer when the weather is
warm. One or two leaves are removed so
that a diagonal cut, about $1\frac{1}{2}$ in. long, can
be made in the stem (2). To keep the cut
open a match stick can be inserted between
the two surfaces (3). To assist good roots to
develop at the cut surfaces the wound can
be treated with a hormone rooting powder
(4). The area is then surrounded with
thoroughly moistened sphagnum moss into
which roots will develop (5). To keep the
moss in a moist condition for some time
it is necessary to enclose it in a piece of
polythene film (6) which is sealed at the top
and bottom with string or adhesive tape (7).
The plant should be kept in a warm part of
the greenhouse where the atmosphere is
moist and watering should be done normally.

Inspect the layer occasionally for signs of
root development and when a good root

4

5

FICUS *continued*

system can be seen through the polythene the new plant can be severed just below the roots (8). As the polythene covering is removed a mass of white roots will be seen twining amongst the moss (9).

Potting. Before the plant is potted the old piece of stem immediately below the roots should be cut off cleanly with a sharp knife (10). Potting may then be done without removing the moss and, depending on the size of the plant, a 5 or 6 in. pot is used (11). Drainage material must be placed in the pot and John Innes Potting Compost No. 1 is a suitable mixture to use. This must be made firm around the roots (12) without being rammed hard. Afterwards a good watering may be given (13) and to help the plant establish itself quickly keep it in a warm, shaded part of the greenhouse. As a result of air-layering a plant in this way one has an attractive and sizeable plant straight away.

Having removed the top of the old plant it will begin to send out side growths (14). When these develop several leaves they, too, in turn can be air-layered (15). These will give rise to slightly smaller plants.

Cuttings. Although air-layering provides a few good plants fairly quickly more plants are obtained if leaf bud cuttings are taken. These consist of small pieces of stem each containing a bud and a leaf. They are placed singly in 2 in. pots containing a mixture of moist peat and coarse sand in equal parts. A propagating box with a temperature of 21°C. (70°F.) is needed and the pots can be plunged in a bed of moist peat inside the box. To prevent damage to the leaves from drips of moisture it is most important to wipe the glass covering each day. When the buds begin to develop and the cuttings make new roots they can be moved to 5 in. pots and grown in 16-18°C. (60-65°F.).

must be grown from corms. These are started into growth in August and will begin to flower in February of the following year.

Good strains of freesia seed are available in a mixture of lovely colours. Seedlings take about nine months to flower and if sown in heat in February or March flowers can be expected in time for Christmas.

Corms. Seven or eight corms can be placed in a 6 in. pot of John Innes Potting Compost No. 1 (2), and covered with about 1 in. of compost. The pots should be put in a cold frame under a thick covering of moist peat. This is to keep the corms cool and so that they can make a good root system. After a period of about six weeks the pots can be removed from the frame and taken into a greenhouse which must be kept well ventilated.

Seed. This germinates best in a temperature of 18°C. (65°F.) and as the seedlings resent disturbance they are usually grown throughout in the same container. 6 in. deep boxes may be used or about six seeds may be sown in a 6 in. pot. As the seed is often erratic in germination some gardeners 'chit' the seed before sowing by mixing it with moist peat in a jar. Kept in a warm place

FREESIA

The freesia with its colourful, scented flowers on thin, wiry stems (1) is one of the most beautiful winter-flowering plants for a cool greenhouse. Anyone with a greenhouse having enough heat to exclude frost and to maintain a temperature of 4-7°C. (40-45°F.) can grow these lovely flowers. The freesia has been developed considerably in the last few years and strains can now be obtained in a variety of delightful shades.

Double Flowers. Forms have also been developed with double flowers that look more like gardenia flowers than freesias. In these the delicious scent has been retained, and, perhaps, improved. At the moment double freesias cannot be obtained by amateurs but it is to be hoped that as stocks increase they will soon be available to everyone.

Methods. There are two methods of growing freesias—seed and corms. Named varieties

there should soon be signs of germination and within a few days the seedlings can be spaced out in pots or boxes of J.I.P.1. During the summer the seedlings are best housed in a well ventilated cold frame or they can be stood outside in a warm, sheltered place (3). The compost in the boxes must never be allowed to dry out and ample water must be given in hot weather in the summer. In late summer feed with a liquid or soluble fertilizer.

The seedling freesias must be taken into the greenhouse in September and their treatment then follows the same pattern as those started from corms. A temperature of 7°C. (45°F.) is adequate but a damp atmosphere must be avoided by careful ventilation. Less water is needed in the autumn and winter but when the soil begins to become dry watering must be done (5).

Staking. Some support is needed to keep the

foliage upright, and thin, twiggy sticks can be used. These are placed around the edge of the pot. Alternatively, thin canes may be used between which raffia can be looped (4). **Resting.** When the flowers fade, watering must continue until the foliage shows signs of yellowing. Water can then be reduced and the pots laid under the greenhouse staging (6). The corms must be kept dry in the summer while they are at rest but in August they can be removed from the pots and started into growth once more in fresh potting soil. Only the largest corms are likely to flower but the smaller ones can be grown separately to produce larger corms for the future.

FUCHSIA

The fuchsia (1) is one of my favourite greenhouse flowers and there can be few plants that give such a long display of bloom in a cool greenhouse for the attention they need. Fuchsias are certainly not difficult to grow and they should be within the capabilities of most amateur gardeners.

There are a host of lovely varieties from which to choose and now that the fuchsia has once more become a popular plant there are several nurserymen specializing in it and young plants can be obtained without difficulty. Apart from growing plants in pots there are numerous varieties with a pendulous habit that are fine for hanging baskets (see page 27).

Some vigorous upright varieties, such as Rose of Castille and Duchess of Albany, can be treated as permanent climbers in the greenhouse if they are planted in a border and a framework of branches is built up under the greenhouse roof—a large plant in full bloom is certainly a magnificent sight. Apart from the hybrid fuchsias there are also some interesting species. *F. corymbiflora* makes a handsome specimen in a large greenhouse. The flowers, which are borne in clusters, are about 3 in. long and deep red in colour. *F. fulgens* is another kind of species which has long and slender reddish flowers.

Cuttings. A good time to take fuchsia cuttings is in July and August to provide plants for flowering in the following summer.

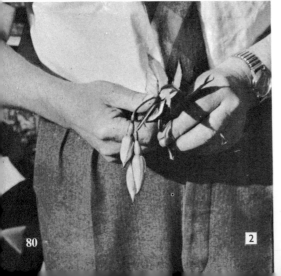

At this time of the year there is plenty of heat in the sun and so temperatures of 16-18°C. (60-65°F.) are not difficult to maintain for rooting the cuttings. Young side shoots, a few inches long, are removed from the plants and any flowers on them should be removed (2). The base of each cutting is trimmed below a joint or node (3) with a sharp knife or razor blade and some of the lower leaves are removed. Cuttings are not difficult to root but a hormone rooting powder can be used with advantage. The base of the cuttings is first dipped in water (4) and then in the powder (5).

Cutting Compost. The cuttings will root satisfactorily in a mixture of equal parts moist granulated peat and coarse sand or a mixture of 1 part good soil, 2 parts moist peat and 3 parts coarse sand can be used.

Three-inch pots are used with a piece of broken pot at the base of each for drainage. The cuttings are inserted around the edge of the pots with a dibber (6) and each pot must be labelled clearly (7) to avoid confusion later on. Give the cuttings a good watering and then put the pots in a propagating box in a warm, shaded part of the greenhouse. Inspect them each day and wipe away condensation that will have formed on the glass.

Another way of rooting the cuttings is to place each pot in a polythene bag which is tied at the top. The bag prevents moisture evaporating but as soon as there are signs of rooting the pots should be taken out.

Potting. Rooted cuttings are first put in 3 in. pots of John Innes Potting Compost No. 1 (8) and grown in a warm, light part

FUCHSIA *continued*

of the greenhouse. Young plants from cuttings must be kept growing slowly throughout the winter and not given a rest as with mature plants. As the plants fill their pots with roots pot on into 5 or 6 in. pots using J.I.P.2 compost.

Pinching. To produce plants with a bushy habit they must be stopped when they are about 6 in. tall by taking out the tips of the main stems (9). This will induce side shoots to form. These, too, in turn must be pinched (10) to build up a good plant. Any flowers that appear are best removed so that the plant makes plenty of growth before the main flowering period begins.

Feeding. Fuchsias grow rapidly in the spring and summer and when they are in the final pots feeds of a liquid or soluble fertilizer should be given each week. This will keep the plants flowering well into the autumn. They must be given ample supplies of water in the summer as in hot weather the soil soon dries out. Light shade can be given from strong sunshine to keep temperatures from rising too high inside the greenhouse. The floors and stagings should also be damped down regularly to create humid conditions around the plants. The atmosphere must never be allowed to become hot and dry as in these conditions red spider mites can spread rapidly.

Standards. To train a standard fuchsia it is best to start with a young plant. It should not be stopped until the main stem has

2

13

reached the desired height—about 3 to 4 ft. A thin cane must be provided to which the main stem can be tied (11) and as the plant develops it should be moved first to a 5 in. pot and later to a 6 or 7 in. pot (12). For the final potting J.I.P.2 compost can be used (13) and firming can be done with a blunt ended rammer (14). As the stem grows in length longer canes are needed (15) so that adequate support can be given with ties of raffia (16) to ensure that the stem grows straight and even.

If a main stem of 3 ft. is required it should be allowed to grow to about $3\frac{1}{2}$ ft. before the tip is taken out (17). This will induce strong side shoots to form in the joints of the leaves and these in turn must be stopped (18) to produce a good 'head'.

14

15

16

83

FUCHSIA *continued*

Resting. Mature fuchsias, whether they are trained as bushes or standards, are given a partial rest in the winter. Very little water is given but the soil should not be allowed to dry out entirely. The plants can be stored in a dry shed or garage and to be sure that frost does not harm the plants straw or bracken can be placed around the stems.

Pruning. This is done in early spring and bush fuchsias are treated in a similar way to standards (these are really a bush on a long stem). The side shoots made in the previous year (19) are cut back hard to within two or three joints of their base (20). Without this pruning plants would become a tangled mass of growth and produce poor flowers.

Repotting. After pruning, potting can be undertaken. The plants are knocked out of their pots and with a pointed stick some of the old potting soil is teased out from the roots (21) so that the plant can be accommodated in the same size pot as the one it was in previously.

The plant is then placed in its new pot (22) in which there is a layer of drainage material in the bottom and the new compost is firmed with a rammer (23).

Standards must be staked carefully and, kept in a warm greenhouse with light overhead sprays of water (24), new growth will soon develop. Afterwards the plants are treated in the same way as young ones. The new growth must be pinched and feeding must be done regularly throughout the season.

Pests. A sharp look out must be kept for insect pests as they can do a lot of damage on fuchsias. Greenfly are usually found congregating on the undersides of the leaves and if they are not controlled black sooty mould soon forms on the leaves. The insects secrete a sugary substance called honeydew on which the black mould develops. Aerosols (25) are available for destroying the insects or spraying can be done with BHC or malathion.

Red spider mites cause a mottling on the foliage which in a bad attack will wither and drop. The mites increase rapidly in hot, dry conditions and, particularly in hot weather, damping down and syringing must be done to create humid conditions. The mites are very small but as soon as they are detected spraying with malathion should be done or the greenhouse can be fumigated with azobenzene.

Capsid bugs, which make small punctures in the leaves and distort them, can also be troublesome but a DDT spray will prevent serious damage.

22

23

25

GLOXINIA

These are popular plants for the summer with handsome flowers (1), velvet-like in texture and in shades of red, blue, rose and white. Apart from the gorgeous flowers the large leaves are also most attractive.

Propagation. Gloxinias are best raised from seed which, if sown in a temperature of 16-18°C. (60-65°F.) in January or February, will produce plants for flowering in mid-summer. The seed is fine and must be sown as thinly as possible. John Innes Seed Compost is suitable and it is not necessary to cover the seed with sifted compost. The seed pots should be stood in a propagating box and the seedlings should appear in 10-14 days. Pricking out must be done in boxes of John Innes Potting Compost No. 1 and in a warm atmosphere, with shade from the sun, growth develops rapidly.

Tubers. Where high temperatures cannot be maintained in the early part of the year gloxinias can be grown from dry tubers started into growth in March or April when temperatures are higher. The tubers

are placed in boxes of sand and peat and kept in a warm shaded part of the green-house. In a moist atmosphere maintained by overhead sprays of water, new growth should soon develop. Before plants grow too large they can be moved to 5 or 6 in. pots (2) and for this potting J.I.P.2 compost can be used. This must be made firm with the fingers (3).

Seedlings. Plants raised from seed and pricked out in boxes are first put in 3½ in. pots (4) of J.I.P.1 compost and as they fill these pots with roots they are moved on to their final 5 or 6 in. pots. When potting it is important to keep the tubers at or slightly above soil level to prevent moisture settling at the base of the leaves. The potting soil must not be made too firm and gentle pressure with the fingers is adequate.

Leaf-cuttings. This method of propagation is not often practised but if one wishes to increase a particularly good seedling it is the best method to adopt. Leaves that are not too large are removed with a piece of

leaf stalk attached, preferably in early summer. Inserted in a bed of peat and sand in a warm propagating box, small tubers soon form and the new plants can then be put individually in small pots.

A variation on this method is to treat the leaves in the same way as those of *Begonia rex*. The main vein on the underside of the leaf is cut at intervals and the leaf is then placed on a mixture of moist peat and sand in a warm propagating box. New tubers and young plants appear from where the cuts were made in the main vein.

During the summer a steady temperature of 16°C. (60°F.) is ideal, rising a little by day with sun heat. Shade must be provided from the sun and a moist atmosphere maintained by frequent damping of the floors and stagings. Moisture must be kept off the developing leaves otherwise they may be badly marked. After potting, little water will be required for a few days but as the plants grow water must be given whenever the soil begins to dry out.

Feeding. To keep the plants growing steadily and to prolong the flowering period for as long as possible feeds with a liquid or soluble fertilizer are beneficial at intervals of 7-10 days.

As the plants come into flower the temperature in the greenhouse can be lowered a little by giving more ventilation whenever possible so that the flowers last longer. As the flowers fade they should be removed (5) to encourage others to develop.

Resting. In late summer when flowering is over, less water can be given although the plants must not be dried off suddenly. To complete their ripening they can be stood in a cold frame (6) but in the autumn they must be returned to a greenhouse to dry off completely. To keep the tubers successfully through the winter they must be stored in a warm, dry place as they are likely to rot if conditions are cold and damp.

GRAPE VINES

Many people have the idea that high temperatures are needed to grow grape vines. This is not altogether true as by choosing varieties carefully it is perfectly feasible to grow a vine in a cold greenhouse (there are, in fact, several varieties that can be grown successfully in the open). The vines themselves are perfectly hardy but some need a longer season than others to ripen the fruit.

Varieties. One of the best grapes for a cold greenhouse is Black Hamburgh and Buckland Sweetwater, a white grape, is another. One of the finest dessert grapes is Muscat of Alexandria but it is not so very easy to grow and must have heat to ripen the fruit.

Vines can be grown in a border inside the greenhouse but where space is limited a large pot or tub can be used if only a few bunches of grapes are needed each year.

Borders. To grow a vine successfully the soil for it must be prepared carefully. The border can be inside or outside the greenhouse. In an outside border the main stem of the vine is passed through a hole in the side of the greenhouse. Good drainage is important and if there is any doubt about this it pays to excavate the soil and lay rubble at the base of the border with tile drains to take surface water away to a lower level. In heavy, sticky soils it is also wise to have an enclosed border with brick or concrete sides so that the roots of the vine cannot penetrate into unsuitable soil. In poorly drained soils vine roots cannot function

properly and troubles such as shanking will develop. Unless the existing soil is good and well drained the border is best filled with a prepared mixture composed of 8 parts decayed turves, 1 part grit or coarse sand, ½ part wood ashes and ¼ part broken charcoal.

Planting. Dormant vines from pots can be planted just before new root growth begins in late winter. The roots should be disentangled so that they can be spread out when planting and covered with about 2 in. of soil; vines must never be planted with their roots in a tight ball. Plants that are raised from 'eyes' in February in a warm greenhouse can be planted direct in borders inside the greenhouse in the summer but as the roots are active they should not be disentangled as with dormant vines.

Pruning. Vines flower and fruit on the new growths made each year and the usual method of pruning in winter is called spur pruning. All the side shoots made in the previous season are cut back in November or December to within one or two buds of their base (1). Afterwards, it is wise to remove all the loose bark on the main stems of the vine by scraping it off carefully with a knife (2) or twisting it off in the hands. The bark must not be stripped off to expose the green rind.

Propagation. The growths removed when pruning can be used to produce young vines. The best and sturdiest shoots can be bundled together and put outside, partly burying them in the soil. In February the shoots are cut up into 'eyes' (3). These consist of pieces of stem each containing a single bud or 'eye'. Trim the cut surfaces with a sharp knife (4) and place the 'eyes' horizontally in sandy soil in 3 in. pots (5). Add a little soil to keep the 'eye' in position (6) but do not cover it completely and place in a propagating box with a temperature of 18°C. (65°F.).

Another method is to lay each 'eye' on a small piece of turf. Pieces of bent wire can be used to hold the 'eyes' in place and the turves are then put on a seed tray stood in a warm propagating box.

New growth soon develops from each bud (7) and good roots appear in about six weeks. The young plants can be moved to a border in the summer or to 5 or 6 in. pots. In the following winter they are repotted in 10 in.

pots if they are to be grown permanently in pots and not in a border.

Potting. After pruning a pot-grown vine in the winter it should be repotted by knocking it out of its pot (8). The drainage material is taken away (9) and some of the old soil is shaken out by loosening it with a hand fork or pointed piece of wood (10). This is done so that the roots can be accommodated comfortably in the same size pot (11). The John Innes Potting Compost No. 3 can be used or a similar mixture to that suggested for vine borders. As the fresh soil is added (12) it must be made firm with a blunt ended rammer (13). After potting a framework should be made with stout stakes or bamboo canes by which the new growths that appear in the spring can be supported. One arrangement is to have a stout central stake with a circular wooden hoop fixed at the top with cross pieces. The new growths are then tied to the hoop and the fruit is well supported.

Stopping. If the new growths that develop in the spring were allowed to grow undisturbed they would soon become a tangled mass and it is necessary to curb the growth. The new shoots should have their tips pinched out two leaves beyond the flower or embryo bunch of fruit (14). Secondary growths will develop as a result of the stopping and these should have their tips taken out at one leaf. Tendrils must also be pinched out (15).

Watering. Vines in pots soon dry out in the summer and watering must be attended to carefully. The soil in a vine border does not become dry so quickly but it should be examined fairly regularly. When watering is done in a border, sufficient should be given so that it penetrates deeply to all the roots.

A mulch of decayed manure over the entire border helps greatly in conserving soil moisture. A top dressing can be given to vines in pots using fresh potting soil and to make space for it a zinc collar can be placed around the rim of the pot. Feeds with a special vine fertilizer must also be given to keep the plants growing well.

Thinning. The developing grapes must be thinned (16) so that each berry has space to develop to a good size. The removal of surplus berries is carried out with a pair of long pointed scissors. The smaller seedless berries are cut out first and then the remainder of the surplus berries can be removed. To avoid touching the berries a small forked stick is useful. It is best to start at the bottom of each bunch and gradually work upwards.

After the fruit has been picked vines in pots can be stood outside to ripen the wood. Watering must continue until the leaves fall and in December it is as well to bring the vines into a greenhouse for pruning and repotting.

HEDERA

There are numerous ivies with ornamental leaves that make excellent pot plants. They have become popular in recent years as house plants and they are certainly not difficult to grow. A great many of the kinds that are available are varieties of the common ivy, *Hedera helix*. One of my favourites is *H. helix* Glacier (1) which has silvery leaves with white margins. Another interesting kind is *H. h. cristata* with crimped edges to the green leaves. *H. canariensis* is more tender than the others but it is a delightful plant with large, cream-edged leaves.

Propagation. Ivies are very easy plants to increase. Two methods are adopted—tip cuttings and leaf bud cuttings. The former are made, a few inches long, from the tips of the stems (2). The lower leaves are removed and each cutting is trimmed below a leaf joint (3). Several of these cuttings can be placed around the edge of a small pot

(4) filled with a mixture of 1 part loam, 2 parts moist peat and 3 parts coarse sand.

A leaf bud cutting consists of a leaf with a small piece of stem; this is cut just above and below the bud in the joint of the leaf. The cuttings are dibbled in pots or boxes containing the same compost as mentioned above.

Cuttings are best taken in the spring and summer and rooting soon occurs if they are placed in a warm propagating box inside the greenhouse. Once rooted the young plants can be put in 2 in. pots of John Innes Potting Compost No. 1 and later moved to $3\frac{1}{2}$ in. pots. Ivies can be grown for some time in small pots if they are well watered and fed. Only when they are really pot bound need they be moved to 5 in. pots.

HIPPEASTRUM

One of my favourite bulbs for the greenhouse is the hippeastrum which is often wrongly called amaryllis. The huge, trumpet-shaped flowers (1) on stiff sturdy stems appear in late winter and spring depending on the temperature that can be given. There are numerous varieties with flowers in varying colours including scarlet, crimson, pink and white.

Good flowering sized bulbs are comparatively expensive but it must be remembered that the bulb will increase and last indefinitely provided it is given good treatment and care is taken.

Potting. A single bulb can be grown in a 5 or 6 in. pot and ample drainage must be provided in the base of the pot. John Innes Potting Compost No. 2 is a suitable mixture to use and the top part of the bulb should be left exposed above the level of the compost. Complete repotting is necessary only every three or four years as the bulbs resent root disturbance, but each year before starting the bulbs into growth, the surface soil should be scraped away (2) so that top dressing can be given with fresh potting compost. This is normally done in February but if early flowers are needed and a temperature of 16°C. (60°F.) can be maintained the bulbs can be started into growth in December or January.

Ideally, the pots are stood on staging with bottom heat (3) maintained with soil warming cables or hot water pipes. Water should be given sparingly until growth is active although the soil must not be allowed to dry out.

Prepared Bulbs. Hippeastrum bulbs can now be obtained that have been specially treated so that they flower early and blooms can be had for Christmas. One variety that is available is called Christmas

HIPPEASTRUM *continued*

Joy and it has bright red flowers. They are available for planting in early November. The bulbs are placed in pots in the normal manner and for Christmas flowering they must be placed in a constant temperature of 21°C. (70°F.). In lower temperatures the flowers will not start to show until mid- or late January.

To prevent the flower stems being damaged by accident it pays to stake them with thin canes and give one or two ties with raffia (4).

After flowering, when the foliage has developed fully, the plants must be looked after well to build up

the bulbs for the following year. They should be placed in a warm part of the greenhouse and given feeds each week with a liquid or soluble fertilizer (5).

Resting. Towards the end of the summer, when the foliage begins to turn yellow, less water can be given and when the soil is dry the pots can be laid on their sides under the staging (6). To ripen the bulbs thoroughly the pots can be stood on the staging where they can receive plenty of sunlight.

This is the method I have practiced successfully for many years but some gardeners feel that the bulbs should not be given a decided rest. The plants are kept in cool conditions in the autumn but the soil is not allowed to dry out entirely, enough being given to keep it just moist so that the bulbs are given a partial rest.

Mealy Bug. This insect with its white woolly covering can be very troublesome on hippeastrums. The insects are usually found in the brown outer coverings of the bulb. When dormant it pays to inspect each bulb thoroughly, removing the brown skin. A brush dipped in diluted malathion or white oil emulsion can be used for destroying the insects.

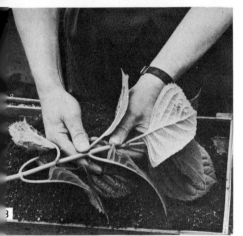

HYDRANGEA

Cuttings. The many garden varieties of *Hydrangea macrophylla* (1) make excellent pot plants for flowering in the spring. For this purpose plants are best raised annually from cuttings taken in March and April.

Cuttings are prepared from strong non-flowering shoots (2). Each cutting should be 4 or 5 in. long. It should be cut cleanly with a sharp knife just below a joint at which leaves grow from the stem (3). The bottom pair of leaves should be removed and the base of the cutting dipped in hormone rooting powder (4). This will adhere more readily if the base of the cutting is first dipped in water. The cuttings are then inserted in a mixture of 1 part medium loam, 2 parts sphagnum peat and 3 parts

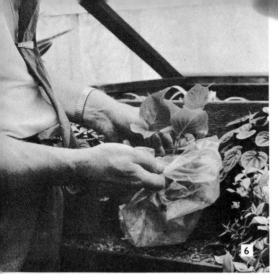

HYDRANGEA *continued*

sand. If a lot of cuttings are to be rooted they may be put in rather deep seed trays, but for a few cuttings, well drained flower pots are better. Insert them about 1 in. deep around the edge of the pot (5).

Growing On. The cuttings need to be rooted in a moderately warm and rather close atmosphere. They may be placed in a propagating box or frame in a temperature of about 16°C. (60°F.), but a simple and effective method if no such facilities are available is to place each pot of cuttings in a polythene bag (6). Slip pot and cuttings right into the bag and place a tie or a rubber band round the top of the bag to close it tightly (7). If the cuttings are well watered in before they are put in the bag, they will probably need no further attention until they are rooted in two or three weeks time. Then they should be carefully tapped out of the pot and separated one from another with as little injury as possible to the roots (8).

Potting. The next step is to pot the rooted cuttings individually in 3 in. pots in John Innes Potting Compost No. 1 (9). If blue flowers are required the chalk or limestone should be omitted from this compost and instead one of the proprietary blueing compounds should be mixed with it according to manufacturer's instructions.

Keep the young hydrangeas in the greenhouse until these first pots are well filled with roots (10) and then move them on into 5 in. pots using J.I.P.2 compost (11) but again minus chalk or limestone and plus blueing compound if blue flowers are required. Note well that for red or pink flowers the chalk or limestone must be used and there must be no blueing compound. Coloured hydrangeas come pink, red or reddish purple in alkaline soil; blue, mauve or bluish-purple in acid soils. White varieties cannot be made either blue or red.

Stopping. When well established in 5 in. pots, the growing tip should be removed from each plant (12). At this stage the plants will be better in a frame than in the greenhouse as they like plenty of air. (13). Keep them well watered throughout as dryness will check growth seriously.

The result of removing the growing tip from each plant will be to make it branch

10

11

2

(14). If cuttings are rooted later than mid-May it will not be wise to stop them in this way as they would make their side growths too late to flower well the following spring. Instead they should be allowed to grow on a single stem and produce only one flower truss per plant. Keep a close watch on the plants for greenfly and spray with menazon or derris if these appear. Also remove any leaves that turn yellow or show signs of decay (14).

By late September it will be wise to keep the lights on the frame at night and a month later they should be back in the greenhouse safe from frost.

One further potting will be required in October, for well grown plants. This will

3

14

97

HYDRANGEA *continued*

be into 7 in. pots and again J.I.P.2 compost will be used with the variations already detailed for these flowers.

Starting. By November the leaves will have fallen and the terminal buds, from which next spring's flowering shoots will be produced, should be well developed (15). It is vital that these shall not be lost by cold or decay during the winter. Little water is needed at this stage, just enough heat to maintain a temperature of 7°C. (45°F.). Soon after the turn of the year the temperature of the house can be raised a little if desired to hasten growth. Very soon growth will restart, leaves will develop and

then, a few weeks later, the clusters of flower buds will be seen at the ends of the branches (16). This is the time to start feeding once a week with a good soluble or liquid fertilizer mixed according to manufacturer's instructions (17). As stems lengthen each must be staked, for the flower heads are heavy (18). Let the stakes slope outwards a little so that the plants are opened up and cut off the stakes just below the flower trusses (19).

Watering. Hydrangeas in growth are thirsty plants and particularly so when they are developing and carrying their very large flower trusses, so at this stage see that they are well watered direct from the spout of the watering can (20).

When the flowers fade they should be cut off together with a little stem (21) to keep the plants compact and encourage further branching. This is also the time to repot the plants either into pots of the same size, in which case some of the old soil must be teased away from the roots, or into slightly larger pots (22). For this use J.I.P.2 compost again plus blueing compound if the aim is to have blue flowers.

During the summer the plants will be better out of the greenhouse which is likely to get too hot and dry for them. They may be placed in a sheltered position outdoors or in a deep frame, and in either case it will help growth to plunge the pots to their rims in sand or peat (23).

PEPEROMIA

These tropical plants are grown primarily for their foliage, always attractive in shape and often variegated in a very ornamental manner as in *Peperomia sandersii* (1) which has leaves striped silver and green. All like warm, humid conditions and thrive in a temperature of around 21°C. (70°F.) in summer, 13-16°C. (55-60°F.) in winter. They need shade in summer and plenty of water both at the roots and in the atmosphere. In winter they need full light, less moisture but they should never be quite dry.

Cuttings. Most peperomias can be increased by cuttings but *P. sandersii* is even more readily increased by pieces of the leaf itself. First a well developed leaf is removed from the plant, stalk and all (1). The leaf is cut up into about four pieces (2) which are then pressed, cut surface downwards, into pots filled with a mixture of sand and peat or with vermiculite (3). The leaves are well watered in (4) and the pot is covered with a sheet of glass (5) and placed in a propagating box or frame in a temperature of 21°C. (70°F.). Roots and new shoots will form at the base of the veins.

POINSETTIA

Poinsettia is the popular name of a tropical American plant botanically named *Euphorbia pulcherrima*. Its flowers are quite insignificant but they are surrounded by large, scarlet leaf-like bracts (1) which are extremely showy and come in the middle of the winter when they are much in demand.

Poinsettias are grown from stem cuttings which are taken in May but first the plants must be cut back after flowering (2) to make them produce side shoots suitable for use as cuttings. The plants are then kept in a rather warm moist atmosphere and the young shoots are removed when 3 or 4 in. long (3). Each is prepared in the usual way as a cutting and the cut ends are dipped in sand to prevent 'bleeding' (4). They are then inserted around the edges of pots filled with a mixture of loam, sand and peat (5). Each pot is clearly labelled (6) for in addition to the ordinary scarlet poinsettia other varieties are available, some with even larger or more richly coloured bracts, one with pink bracts and another with white bracts.

Another way of propagating poinsettias is to cut up the stems, made in the previous year, into pieces about 2 in. long. Treated in a similar way to ordinary cuttings they soon form roots.

Late Cuttings. Plants raised from cuttings in May and June will grow to a height of

4

6

POINSETTIA *continued*

about 6 ft. before the end of the year and if smaller plants, about 12 in. tall, are required, cuttings can be taken in August. Three small plants can be put in a 5 or 6 in. pot.

Rooting. The pots containing the cuttings should be placed in a propagating box or frame with bottom heat of 21°C. (70°F.) or more. When well rooted the cuttings are potted individually, first into 3½ in. pots and later into 6 or 8 in. pots. For the first potting John Innes Potting Compost No. 1 should be used but the stronger No. 2 compost may be used for the second potting.

At first the plants should be grown on in a warm rather humid greenhouse, but as they become established they can be accustomed gradually to a lower temperature so that during August and early September they can stand in a frame. Bring back to the greenhouse before there is any danger of frost and maintain a temperature of 16-18°C. (60-65°F.)—more if early 'flowers' are required. For the finest development of the bracts plants should be restricted to one stem each (7) and should be fed once a week from late September until flowering time with a soluble or liquid fertilizer.

Water very carefully as dryness at the roots at any time will cause the leaves to turn yellow and drop. Fluctuations in temperature will also cause the leaves to fall.

After flowering old plants can be cut back and potted unless it is preferred to rely on fresh stock from cuttings.

7

PRIMULAS

The primulas grown in greenhouses are exotic relatives of our native primrose and cowslip. They are mainly winter flowering and they are ideal plants for the amateur as they do not require much heat.

The three most popular species are *Primula obconica* (1), *P. malacoides* (2) and *P. sinensis* (3).

P. obconica has the longest season of flowers and often goes on intermittently throughout the year, but it is as a winter and early spring flowering plant it is chiefly valued. Colours available are pink, salmon, red, blue and white. The leaves cause a rash on the skin of some people allergic to this plant.

P. malacoides has smaller, more numerous flowers borne in elegant sprays, one whorl of flowers above another. The colour range has been more limited, pink, rose and carmine but lately new shades of lilac, violet, blue and salmon-scarlet have been added. This is certainly one of the most valuable winter flowering plants for the amateur.

P. sinensis has larger flowers and a greater range of colour and flower forms, one type

with more star-shaped flowers being distinguished as *P. sinensis stellata*. Another form with fringed flowers is sometimes called *P. sinensis fimbriata*. *P. sinensis* in all its forms is a little more difficult to grow than either *P. obconica* or *P. malacoides*.

Cultivation. The cultivation of all three kinds of greenhouse primula is similar but there are differences in sowing time. Seed of *P. obconica* and *P. sinensis* is best sown in March or April and *P. malacoides* in late June or early July. All need a temperature of 16°C. (60°F.) for quick germination. The seed is small and should be covered very lightly. Sometimes germination is erratic and in that case it is wise to prick out seedlings a few at a time as they become large enough to handle. For both seed sowing and pricking out the John Innes Seed Compost is suitable. It is wise to cover seed pans or pots with both glass and paper until germination takes place but then the seedlings must have full light to keep them sturdy. The soil must also be kept moist throughout.

Seedlings. Prick out into other seed pans or boxes (4) spacing all seedlings about $1\frac{1}{2}$ in. apart. Keep in the same temperature and shade from strong direct sunshine. Alternatively, seedlings of *P. obconica* can be pricked out $2\frac{1}{2}$ in. apart and one potting can be omitted. The first potting should be done when the leaves are touching in the boxes and before the young plants get checked by starvation (5). It will be into 3 in. pots if the seedlings were pricked off closely, into 5 in. pots if they were widely spaced. Lift and separate very carefully and use the John Innes Potting Compost No. 1 for this first potting. Run in this compost evenly all round each plant (6) and firm it lightly with the fingers (7). Primulas do not like very hard soil.

7

8

Frames. In high summer the plants will be better in a frame than a greenhouse which is apt to get too hot and dry for them, but if no frame is available the glass should be permanently shaded on the sunny side, plenty of ventilation given and paths and stages frequently wetted to maintain a moist atmosphere. If in frames it will help to plunge the pots to their rims in sand, ashes or peat.

Those plants that were potted into 3 in. pots should be moved on into 5 in. pots as soon as the smaller pots are comfortably filled with roots. For this second potting the J.I.P.2 compost is suitable.

Watering. By the end of September the plants must be back in the greenhouse again. From this stage onwards they require careful watering. Apply the water direct to the soil from the spout of the watering can (8). Primulas need plenty of moisture but not on their leaves in autumn and winter where it is likely to encourage grey mould, a disease to which they are rather subject, especially in a cold, damp atmosphere. Grey mould is less likely to appear at temperatures above 13°C. (55°F.), but perfectly good primulas can be grown at a minimum of 7°C. (45°F.) if care is taken to prevent damp. If trouble should develop pick off any leaves that show signs of decay (10). If yellowing of the leaves occurs sprinkle calcined sulphate of iron around the base of the plant (9).

As soon as the 5 in. pots are well filled with roots feeding should commence. This is particularly necessary with *P. malacoides*. Use a good soluble or liquid fertilizer mixed according to manufacturer's instructions and repeat every week or 10 days up to and during the time that the plants are in flower.

9

10

REGAL PELARGONIUMS

These splendid plants are related to the familiar garden Geranium but have large flowers often in two colours (1). They make large and showy pot plants to bloom in spring and early summer and are particularly easy to grow.

Cuttings. Regal pelargoniums are grown from cuttings of firm young growth which can be rooted at any time in spring or summer but for convenience are usually taken in July when the plants have finished flowering (2). Non-flowering shoots 3-5 in. in length are required: each is cut cleanly at the base immediately below a leaf (3). The lowest leaf or sometimes, if the leaves are close together, the two lowest leaves are then removed and the base of the cutting is dipped in hormone rooting powder (4). The cuttings are best rooted in pots in a mixture of 1 part medium loam, 2 parts peat and 3 parts coarse sand and a little extra sand should be spread over the top of this compost in the pot (5). Then, as the cuttings are dibbled in around

the side of the pot (6) a little of this sand will fall into each hole and lie at the base of the cutting so giving improved drainage and aeration and assisting in the rooting of the cuttings. Keep one variety to a pot and label each pot clearly (7).

Rooting. The cuttings should be well watered in from a watering can fitted with a fine rose turned downwards so that the spray of water is directed down on to the compost so settling it firmly around the cuttings (8). If shaded from direct sunshine, well watered, and syringed with water once or twice daily the cuttings will root on the open bench of a greenhouse. Alternatively they may be placed in a propagating box or frame in which less watering and spraying will be needed.

When well rooted the cuttings should be potted individually in 3 or 3½ in. pots in the John Innes Potting Compost No. 1 but for later potting it will be better to use the stronger J.I.P.2.

Grow on the young plants in a light, airy greenhouse in a temperature around 10-13°C. (50-55°F.) though it will not matter if it falls occasionally five or 10 degrees lower. Water in autumn and winter sufficiently to keep the soil moist but never sodden but in spring increase the water supply considerably. The plants must be moved on into larger pots (9) as soon as the smaller

ones become comfortably filled with roots. Young plants will probably need the 6 or 7 in. size by flowering time the first spring but older plants may easily need larger pots.

Feeding. As flowering time approaches feeding should commence with a soluble or liquid fertilizer mixed according to manufacturer's instructions (10). Each plant should be well watered with this once a week in place of ordinary water (11). Throughout this period see that the plants are well supplied with water for they make a lot of foliage and carry many flowers (12) and therefore use a good deal of water. Note that in the preceding picture (11) the plants have been stood on inverted flower pots to bring them closer to the glass. This might not be necessary in a small greenhouse but it is important that

pelargoniums should have plenty of light. The thimble on the end of a bamboo cane in this same picture is used to tap the pots in which the pelargoniums are growing. If they give a hollow or ringing sound the soil is too dry; if the note is dull and heavy the soil is moist.

Pruning. After flowering the plants should be cut back quite severely (13) as if left unpruned they tend to grow too tall and weak. From this time until September they are best stood in a sunny sheltered place outdoors or in a deep frame and, until new growth appears, the water supply should be considerably reduced.

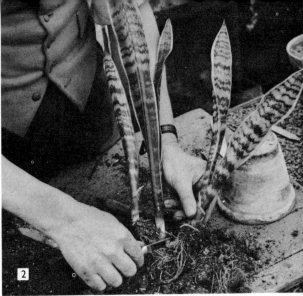

SANSEVIERIA

The type most commonly cultivated is *S. trifasciata laurentii* (1) which is often called Bow-string Hemp. The erect, sword-shaped leaves are mottled and have two yellow bands running the length of the leaves close to the edges. It has become a popular house plant although it grows best in a warm greenhouse.

Propagation. Sansevierias have a suckering habit and the best way to increase plants is to divide them in the spring. Rooted off-sets can be detached with a sharp knife (2) and placed in 3 in. pots (3). A suitable soil mixture to use is John Innes Potting Compost No. 1 (4), which should be firmed evenly with the fingers (5). After potting, the plants must be kept in the warmest part of the greenhouse to encourage them to make new roots rapidly.

Watering. This must be done carefully and the compost must not be kept over wet otherwise rotting is likely to occur. In winter, when temperatures are low, allow the compost to dry out before giving water. In summer give more water but wait till the soil is almost dry.

1

SCHIZANTHUS

Poor Man's Orchid and Butterfly Flower are two common names given to this lovely half-hardy annual which can, provide a delightful display in the spring or summer in a frost-free greenhouse. There are several fine seed strains in colours ranging from red, pink and crimson to mauve and purple. The large flowered kinds make a magnificent show potted in 6 or 7 in. pots (1) but the dwarf Bouquet strains are also excellent.

Sowing. Seed can be sown at different times according to when one wishes to have flowers. It is, however, usually sown in early September to provide plants for flowering in the following May but seed can also be sown in February, March or April if flowers

3

4

are required in the summer. Sowing can be done in John Innes Seed Compost spacing out the seed to prevent over crowding of the seedlings and for the September sowing the pots can be placed in a cold frame as high temperatures are not required for germination.

Potting. As soon as the seedlings can be handled they should be moved individually to 3 in. pots of John Innes Potting Compost No. 1 (2). To keep them growing sturdily they like cool conditions close to the glass and a good place for the young plants is on a shelf under the greenhouse roof.

A further move to 5 in. pots can be given in November as the roots begin to fill the 3 in. pots (3). For this potting use J.I.P.2 (4) which will contain sufficient nutrients to keep the plants growing slowly and steadily through the winter.

Watering. Schizanthus are likely to damp off in the winter if the soil is kept too wet when the weather is cold. Watering, therefore, must be done sparingly but when the soil begins to dry out more water must be given. As the days become warmer in the spring growth accelerates and more water is required.

Although the plants will be happy where the temperature does not fall below 4-7°C. (40-45°F.) they will not do well in damp, stuffy conditions. The roof ventilators

8

c

SCHIZANTHUS *continued*

must be opened a little whenever possible for at least a few hours each day unless the weather is foggy.

Stopping. To produce plants with a well branched, bushy habit the tips of the main stems can be taken out (5) when they are about 6 in. tall. This will encourage side shoots to develop.

Staking. Adequate support must be given to the stems as the plants grow in size. At first a short split cane is sufficient but once side growths develop, twiggy sticks are needed which are inserted around the edge of each pot (6).

Final Potting. In February, plants from an early autumn sowing should be ready for their final pots—6 or 7 in. pots. The compost can be J.I.P.2 and it should be firmed evenly with a wedge shaped stick (7).

When established in their final pots the tips of the side stems can be removed (8) to keep the plants neat and compact. Staking can also be completed at this stage. I put three canes in each pot (9) and around them make raffia ties (10) at intervals to keep the growths in place. Although this does not appear very attractive at first the new foliage soon conceals the canes and raffia.

Feeding. In early spring growth is made rapidly and before the plants fill their final pots with roots, feeds should be given with a liquid or soluble fertilizer. Yellowing of the foliage is a sign that the plants need extra nourishment but feeding should begin before this stage is reached.

A watch must be kept for signs of greenfly as they can soon spoil a good plant. The insects are not difficult to destroy as there are numerous good insecticides on the market. There is a systemic insecticide that is simply watered on the soil or fumigation can be carried out with a BHC smoke pellet or with nicotine shreds.

10

SOLANUM

Commonly called Winter Cherry, *Solanum capsicastrum*, with bright red berries (1) is at its best in the winter and it is very popular at Christmas. It is not a difficult plant to grow and it will succeed in a greenhouse with a minimum temperature of 7°C. (45°F.).

Propagation. Plants can be kept from year to year but new ones may be raised from the seeds which are found inside the berries (3). These are removed carefully (2) ready for sowing in February or early March. This can be done in small pots of John Innes Seed Compost made level and firmed by even pressure with the base of a pot. The seeds are large enough to be spaced out individually (4) and they should be covered lightly with fine soil (5) and firmed (6).

After a good watering each pot should be labelled clearly and covered with a piece of glass (7). Stood in a propagating box with a temperature of 16-18°C. (60-65°F.) germination soon takes place and the glass must be removed.

Potting. When the seedlings are about 1 in. high they should be moved to 3 in. pots of John Innes Potting Compost No. 1 and as they fill these pots with roots they can be potted on to 5 or 6 in. pots.

To encourage a bushy habit the tip of each plant should be pinched out when it is a few inches tall and in the summer further pinching of the side growths can be done to keep the plants bushy and compact.

From early June until September the plants can be put outside in a frame or they may be removed from their pots and planted out in a warm, sunny border of good soil.

SOLANUM *continued*

Pollination. Amateur gardeners often tell me that the flowers on their solanums do not set berries. To ensure a good set I spray my plants with water each day when they are in flower (8). If this is done plenty of berriers should form.

Plants that are kept in pots in the summer need to be fed each week with a liquid or soluble fertilizer and in hot weather they need copious supplies of water.

Housing. In September the plants must be taken into a light place in the greenhouse (9). Those that are planted outside must be potted firmly in 6 in. pots and kept warm and close until they have settled down in the pots.

STOCKS

Few people seem to grow stocks (1) in their greenhouses but they are excellent for a cool greenhouse in late winter. The Beauty of Nice type are particularly recommended for cultivation under glass and there are numerous varieties from which to choose with rose, pink, violet, salmon and white flowers. There are also varieties which, by selecting only the lighter coloured seedlings, will produce entirely double flowers.

Sowing. Seed is best sown in July or August in pots or boxes of John Innes Seed Compost. These can be stood in a shaded cold frame until germination takes place. The seedlings must be pricked out (2 and 3) in boxes of John Innes Potting Compost No. 1 and kept in a frame so that they have cool, airy conditions. Before colder weather arrives they should be taken into a greenhouse with a temperature of about 7°C. (45°F.).

Potting. Young plants can be put first in 3 in. pots and later moved to 5 in. pots (4)

of J.I.P.2 compost. During the winter they must be kept in a light place and the roof ventilators should be opened a little whenever possible to avoid damp and stuffy conditions. Water must be given sparingly and only when the soil is dry—over wet conditions will cause the plants to damp off.

TOMATOES

Most amateur gardeners like to grow a few tomato plants in their greenhouses. The plants can be grown in borders of good soil, in large boxes or pots, or in bottomless pots if the ring culture system is followed. There are numerous varieties from which to choose but two good ones are Moneymaker and Ailsa Craig. Yellow varieties have good flavour and they are well worth a trial.

To be able to raise plants from seed successfully a steady temperature of 16°C. (60°F.) is needed in the greenhouse. Commercial growers sow their seed in December for early crops but the cost of heating is very high and most amateurs will wait until February or March before sowing their seed. Where it is not possible to maintain a sufficiently high temperature it is best to buy plants from a good local nursery.

Sowing. The seed can be sown in boxes of John Innes Potting Compost No. 1, the surface of which should be made firm and level (1). I believe in spacing out the seed when sowing (2) so that each seedling has plenty of space when it appears. If the seed is sown too thickly the seedlings become drawn and spindly (4); in this state they are likely to damp off.

The seed should be covered with a layer of fine compost after sowing (3) and to prevent loss of moisture, boxes are covered with glass and paper. Germination should take place in just over a week when the coverings must be removed from the box which is best stood on a shelf close to the light to keep the seedlings sturdy.

Potting. The seedlings must not be left in the boxes too long and the first potting is in 3½ in. pots (5) of J.I.P.1 compost taking care to handle the seedlings by their leaves

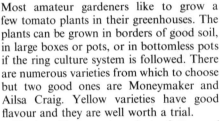

and not the stems which bruise easily. Instead of using pots, soil blocks may be used.

Ring Culture. This is an excellent system of growing tomatoes. If plants are grown in a border of soil year after year they are likely to decline in vigour and cropping capacity. This is because of a condition known as soil sickness which can be put right only by sterilizing the soil with steam or renewing the soil entirely. This is an arduous and expensive business which can be avoided by growing plants on the ring culture system.

The plants are grown in bottomless pots or rings (6) which are stood on a base of coarse weathered cinders, coarse sand or $\frac{3}{4}$ in. grade ballast. It is most important that cinders are well weathered before use to remove sulphur deposits. If this is not done it will lead to troubles later on and the plants will not develop a vigorous root system. The rings must not be put too close together and a spacing of 18 in. apart should be allowed. They are partly filled with J.I.P.3 compost (7) and before the tomatoes completely fill the 3 in. pots with roots they are planted in the rings (8) so that the level of the compost is about 1 in. below the rim of the ring.

Before planting make sure that the plants are well watered. Two root systems are encouraged to develop with ring culture— fine feeding roots in the rings and coarse roots in the aggregate. To make the plants produce roots as quickly as possible into the aggregate, water should be given sparingly at first but after 7-10 days the aggregate can be drenched with water each day and a little water can be given to the rings. Some gardeners find that their plants do not make roots into the aggregate satisfactorily. This is often because too much water is given to the rings after planting and as a result the roots do not go in search of moisture.

Feeding. As soon as the first fruits form, feeding with a liquid or soluble fertilizer, specially recommended for ring culture, is carried out in the rings at intervals of a week and from then on water is given only to the aggregate (9) and liquid feeds (10) are given to the rings.

Plants that are grown in the conventional manner in borders or boxes also need

TOMATOES *continued*

feeding (11). The time when feeding should begin does depend on the growth of the plants but it is usually needed by the time the second truss has formed. There are several excellent proprietary tomato fertilizers on the market.

Supports. Whether tomatoes are grown in borders of soil or in rings they need adequate support. One method is to insert a hooked galvanized wire close to each plant. Lengths of soft string are tied, not too tightly, from the wires (12) to overhead supports on the greenhouse roof. As the plants develop the string is carefully wound round the main stem (13).

Plants that are grown in large pots or boxes on the greenhouse staging can be supported with stout bamboo canes and the main stems tied loosely to the canes.

Side Shoots. Tomatoes are grown as cordons

with one main stem and the side shoots that form in the joints of the leaves must be removed as soon as they can be handled. This is most easily done by bending the shoot over with finger and thumb (14) when it should break away cleanly at its base.

Temperatures. To grow tomatoes well they must have a minimum temperature of 13°C. (55°F.) at night rising higher by day. In lower temperatures growth is made slowly and there will not be a good set of fruit. During the summer the roof ventilators must be opened gradually as the temperature rises and in very hot weather it may be necessary to give light shade to prevent over hot conditions inside the greenhouse.

Pollination. To ensure that the flowers set fruit satisfactorily it pays to spray over the

plants each day with water. This is best done in the middle of the morning when the ventilators can be closed for half an hour so that the air becomes really humid around the plants. Afterwards the ventilators should be reopened gradually as tomatoes must have a good buoyant atmosphere. In a poorly ventilated greenhouse serious diseases are likely to develop.

Disorders. A great many of the troubles that affect tomatoes arise because of cultural faults. Blossom end rot, which causes black sunken areas at the base of the fruit, occurs if the plants have been allowed to dry out at some stage. Leaf-mould is a disease that is common in poorly ventilated greenhouses and apart from improving ventilation spraying with a copper fungicide is necessary as soon as the first signs of the disease are noticed. White fly may appear despite good cultivation but the insects can be destroyed as soon as they are noticed with one or two fumigations with DDT smoke bombs.

TULIPS

Apart from daffodils and hyacinths, pots of tulips (1) add much colour to a spring display in the greenhouse. The types that are used for this purpose are the Early Singles and Doubles as well as Mendel and Triumph tulips. These can be had in flower early in the year but most Darwin tulips cannot be had in bloom earlier than the middle of March. Good bulb nurseryman's catalogues indicate suitable varieties for early work but a few well tried varieties are: Brilliant Star (Early Single), Couleur Cardinal (Early Single), Vuurbaak (Double), Orange Nassau (Double), Olaf (Mendel), Edith Eddy (Triumph) and William Copland (Darwin).

Potting. For very early tulips the bulbs should be placed in pots in September and for later varieties potting can be done in early October. John Innes Potting Compost No. 1 may be used and about five bulbs can be accommodated

in a 5 in. pot (2). The compost should be firmed gently and just cover the bulbs (3).

To enable the bulbs to make a good root system they must be kept in a cool, dark place for several weeks. A well drained position outside, close to a hedge or a north facing wall, is ideal (4). The pots must be labelled with the names of the varieties. A good watering should be given (5) and the pots are covered with a 6 in. layer of sand or moist peat (6).

The bulbs can be removed in batches, to provide a succession of flowers from early December, and placed in a darkened cold frame to lengthen the stems and draw the buds out of the bulbs. They may then be taken into a warm greenhouse in a partially shaded position with a temperature of about 13°C. (55°F.). Higher temperatures can be given when the buds are well developed.

Watering. The soil must not be allowed to dry out at any stage

and watering should continue after the flowers have faded and until the foliage withers. Water can then be withheld and the bulbs stored for planting in good soil outside in the autumn. The bulbs cannot be used for forcing in the following year but planted outside they will build up again.

Species Tulips. Apart from the popular tulip hybrids there are many delightful small growing species that are excellent in a cold greenhouse or frame. Most of them are hardy and grow well in a rock garden but with the protection of a greenhouse or frame the blooms can open without any damage from the weather. There are numerous varieties of *T. kaufmanniana*, the Water Lily tulip. The true species has cream coloured petals that are tinged with red on the outside. *T. praestans* has several orange-red flowers on each stem and *T. chrysantha* is a delightful delicate species with yellow petals on the outside and rose-red on the inside.

These are but a few of the many interesting species that can be grown in pots. The bulbs are placed in gritty soil in early autumn and taken into the greenhouse later. when they have made good roots. No heat must be given and most kinds will start flowering in March.

4

5

6

ZONAL PELARGONIUMS

Although grown mainly as a summer bedding plant the Zonal Pelargonium (1), which is incorrectly but commonly called Geranium (it is unfortunate that Geranium is the botanical name for an entirely different plant), also makes a fine pot plant in a frost-free greenhouse. The word zonal is used for these pelargoniums as most varieties have a darker zone on the leaves.

Cuttings. These are usually taken in the spring or late summer. Firm shoots should be chosen, the lower leaves removed and each cutting trimmed below a joint at the base (2). Several cuttings can be placed around the edge of a 5 in. pot or they may be put singly in small pots of sandy soil. Stood on the greenhouse staging rooting soon occurs and the young plants should be moved to $3\frac{1}{2}$ in. pots (3). Those taken in late summer can be kept in these pots for the winter and moved to 5 and 6 in. pots in the spring and summer (4). To produce plants with a bushy habit the tips of the stems should be nipped out. Later the side shoots also need to be stopped.

Winter Flowers. The plants will be in flower in the following summer but if the flower buds are pinched out until September they can be had in flower during the winter. These plants are best stood outside in a sunny spot in the summer. They soon fill their pots with roots and use up all the goodness in the soil. Feeding is therefore necessary every week with a liquid or soluble fertilizer and watering must be done regularly. Before the end of September the plants must be returned to a frost-free greenhouse which should be ventilated freely whenever the weather allows.

Repotting. It is not necessary to raise new plants each year. The stems of old plants can be cut back in the spring. Some of the old potting soil should be shaken from the roots so that the plants can be put in 5 or 6 in. pots.

INDEX